MW00977543

TWISTS

TWISTS

A collection of shorts with surprise endings

Good things can come in small packages.

Alexa Anne Kempson

ISBN-13: 978-1502380104

ISBN-10: 1502380102

i

ALEXA ANNE KEMPSON

DEDICATION

I dedicate this book of shorts to the shortest people I know and love, my grandchildren: Maija, Elyssa, Anna Sophia, Albert and Dashiell. In honor of them I begin with my poem 'specially for little people. (The rest of the book, adults, enjoy!)

Timothy T. Me

I got up one morning and
Said with a stretch,
"What a nice day
For one sided catch."

I had no choice
For two-sided or three;
With no brother or sister
I must play with me.

I used to be sad
About this lone situation,
No games could be held
Without my participation.

TWISTS

So sad 'til that morning
At quarter to nine
I looked in the mirror
At a face just like mine.

Same eyes, nose and chin,
Ears, hair and teeth,
But his lips were moving
And they were talking to me.

"Can I play with you?
My time is quite free.
My name, by the way, is
Timothy T. Me.

We look just alike,
We're just the same tall.
'Cept grownups looking my way
Can't see me at all.

But games we can play 'em,
A lot, we two –
Timothy T. Me and
Timothy T. You."

So from that moment on
I was never alone.
We played in our yard.
We played in our home.

We played in the park.

ALEXA ANNE KEMPSON

We rode on our bikes.
We camped in the dark
And went on long hikes.

He listened quite well
When we sat in our tree
And I told all my jokes
To Timothy T. Me.

Quarrels that we had
Were few and not long.
Timothy T. Me
Always knew he was wrong.

We were never apart
(I could never quite lose 'im)
If being alone
Was what I was choosin'.

But all in all,
What great thing to be
Playing all day
With Timothy T. Me.

A great thing, that is,
'Til one day last week
Dad, coming home,
Kissed me on the cheek.

After several more kisses
And one hug or two,

TWISTS

He said, "Have I got
Some great news for you!

You won't be alone now,
Thanks to your mother
Who's just given birth to
YOUR NEW BABY BROTHER!"

I raced up the stairs
To tell Timothy T. Me
That in the near future
I wouldn't be free.

But lo! And behold!
In the mirror I stared
As Timothy T. Me
Vanished into thin air.

"I really must go,"
He said looking blue.
"My mother gave me
A new brother, too."

ALEXA ANNE KEMPSON

CONTENTS

TWISTS

CONTENTS

ALEXA ANNE KEMPSON

ACKNOWLEDGMENTS

I would like to acknowledge the Walton-DeFuniak Springs Library Writers Group. Each week a writer's prompt was given to us in order to challenge our creativity and writing skills. These were wonderful tools and can be found at: http://creativewritingprompts.com/#

For some reason my initial stories all had surprise endings. I decided to maintain that as a constant for the year. I have always had a fondness for twists and turns in books so it was only natural for me to publish the 'twisted' stories here.

Several of these stories appear elsewhere in publications by our writers' group. "The Crystal Indian" appears in *Tales From Beyond: An Anthology of the Supernatural*. "A Fortunate Misfortune," "Where He Sat," and "Winds of Change" appear in *The Writer's Prompt Anthology*. All have been re-edited for this publication.

Alexa Anne Kempson

September 2014

TWISTS

CHAPTER ONE

TO EACH HIS OWN

"Love looks not with the eyes, but with the mind,

And therefore is winged Cupid painted blind."

William Shakespeare

A Midsummer's Night Dream

Prompt

Brandi Engler and Greg Sampson meet a week before his wedding. One of them is allergic to almonds. Write their story.

"That's not fair!" Brandi Engler jumped as high as her short frame allowed, trying to catch a particularly vicious toss from her stepbrother Greg Sampson.

"Since when have I ever been fair to you, Bottle." He shouted after her as she ran to retrieve the high thrown ball.

Brandi aimed low hoping for payback. She hated it when Greg used that nickname he gave her so long ago. After all, she was going through what she considered her fat, awkward stage then. "You're shaped just like a chunky Coke bottle," he would say and then he would make that va-va voom hourglass shape with his hands. She had showed him. It was a model thin, but athletic Brandi that propelled the ball right towards his groin with unerring accuracy.

Greg snatched it from certain agony as Brandi yelled out, "Oops!"

"Time out," he made the "T" sign and the pair strolled over to the cooler for a couple of beers. They seemed a natural couple and, but for the fact that his mom had married her dad fifteen years ago, they might have ended up that way Greg had often thought. Brandi had been a little blond ball of fire whose only joy was keeping up with her older stepbrother and his friends. Her tomboy phase had ungracefully given way to her adolescent 'Bottle' stage. But all was well now. She was a petite, gorgeous blond and for some years had had her pick of any guy she wanted. He pushed down a guilty thought as he had often done for the past decade.

"Just think in a week you will have a new sister." He grinned broadly as he reached into the cooler and pulled out a couple of cans. They sat, side by side, popped the tabs and took a long satisfying drink.

"Nothing like a cold one to ease the tension." Greg said as he dug his feet into the sand and gazed at the emerald waters of the Gulf of Mexico.

"Not nervous about the honeymoon, are you? I'm sure Shelley has low expectations. Don't worry, you'll improve with time." Brandi teased.

"Very funny." He punched her arm, took a swig and stared. "Sis..."

11

This form of address signaled seriousness, so Brandi cradled her beer in her hands and looked thoughtfully at the sand to await her brother's next words.

"I've never thanked you for introducing me to Shelley. I never thought I would find anyone like her. So... Thanks. I know it sounds corny, but it's the way I feel." One of those long pauses followed. While Greg stared at the water, Brandi swallowed a long draught and waited.

"She's the kind of girl you naturally want to protect." he continued, and then to ward off any teasing from Brandi, he quickly followed his sentiment with, "Okay, I'm a macho, sexist pig."

Surprisingly, instead of agreeing with his self-assessment, Brandi replied softly, "I know what you mean."

Each pursued his and her own thoughts as they watched the gulf. The light on the water reflected the sun's setting behind them in a parfait of pinks and oranges.

Brandi remembered her first encounter with Shelley. Pearse Middle School, her Bottle stage. Brandi had blossomed over the summer after sixth grade; consequently she suffered from the leers of hormone-fueled boys as she maneuvered the halls her first day of classes as a seventh grader. It was worse for Shelley. The new girl was excruciatingly skinny, tall and gawky, with a ponytail to her butt and owl-like glasses. Nicknamed 'Toothbrush,' Shelley readily invited signs reading 'Kick me' to be stuck on her back.

Brandi had never thought of herself as the defender of the defenseless, but something had risen up inside her that day. For the next two years, the Bottle protected the Toothbrush. And so they were known until ninth grade when they reversed roles, for the Bottle became more of a Toothbrush and the Toothbrush, more of a Bottle.

It was harder to look after her then. Boys, with all the typical accompanying distractions and dangers, had crept into their relationship. That was inevitable. Greg was enough older that he never really knew Shelley during the middle and high school years of friendship. It was at the beach after her first year at FSU that Greg formally met Shelley. Brandi hadn't really meant to introduce them; it had just happened. But she silently accepted his thanks anyway.

Parallel, the step siblings sat, but with nothing like parallel thoughts.

Greg was recalling the day he, Brandi and Shelly were at a party at FSU. All he could think about was getting back to his room with Shelley after the party, but he did his best to join in things as though he and Shelley were not eager, new lovers. His concentration on this task was intense enough that he scooped up a handful of nuts and popped them into his mouth without checking. Almonds. Three hours and one emergency room visit later. He awoke to two pairs of eyes: Shelley's, concerned and still dilated with fear and Brandi's dominated by – what? Chastisement? Frustration? Confusion? He was never sure. It was Shelley who had kept calm and gotten him to the ER. Maybe he was the one who needed protecting.

Brandi broke the silence. "To each his own, Big Brother. We are all meant for someone."

They gathered their belongings and headed for the car.

***

"I now pronounce you Man and Wife."

Brandi rolled these words around in her brain. "I wonder why they don't say 'Husband and Wife?' or 'Man and Woman?' She was withstanding boredom as best she could while the photographer snapped photos of the wedding party. "What a loss," her thoughts rambled on as she mechanically smiled for the photographer. "My stepbrother with my best friend." Then, aloud, "Cheese!" she returned to her thoughts. "Photos, unending; dinner, an hour or so; toasts and dancing, another hour or so. So two and a half hours, maybe, then the cake. Then it will be almost over. Oh, there's an attractive prospect over there. No, there's only one person for me."

***

Three hours later Brandi stood close by the newlyweds as the cake was cut. She watched intently as Greg and Shelley paused, each with a piece of cake in hand, poised to shove it into the other's mouth. Snap, snap, snap went the photographer. The newlyweds shoved. Brandi focused first and foremost on Shelley who was beaming, laughing and wiping icing from her lips. As she stared, the bride's expression changed to one of horror. Immediately, Brandi rushed over to catch the falling figure of her stepbrother.

"Call 911." Brandi screamed at no one in particular. She knew there was no hope. Greg was struggling to breathe. He looked at Brandi incredulously. She bent low to his face.

"The icing." he gasped.

"Almond. In a big way. My last minute recommendation." She whispered cradling his head as any adoring sister would.

Greg was fading fast. He couldn't speak, but Brandi read "why?" in his eyes before they closed forever.

"To each his own, Big Brother, and Shelley belongs to me."

CHAPTER TWO

A TALE OF TWO SITTIES

"If animals could speak, the dog would be a blundering outspoken fellow…"

Mark Twain

Prompt

Use all of these words in a poem: crash, crumpled paper, straw, gravel, ochre.

15

ALEXA ANNE KEMPSON

I heard a crash and turned around

To see what she'd done this time.

With her impish ways and legs unsound,

I guessed at what I would find.

My ice tea glass with straw and ice

Were shattered on the floor;

"You're such a scamp! You'll pay the price!

I'll get you now!" I roared.

She didn't move or bat an eye

But stood amid the mess,

Willfully determined not to fly,

My precious young princess!

I grabbed a piece of crumbled paper

Of nasty yellow ochre.

I rolled it up into a taper,

So I might gently poke her.

Her dignity unruffled

She headed for the door.

Her comments discreetly muffled,

TWISTS

I could stand no more.

Out the door, across the porch,

My paper weapon flailing.

Brandishing it like an unlit torch

I forgot to grab the railing.

My weapon of choice was soon unraveled

And turned into a fan

I pitched headlong onto the gravel

Sitting sorely on my can.

She sat serenely and cocked her head

No doubt of her concern.

Dogs will be dogs, it is said

It's masters who need to learn.

CHAPTER THREE

A MATTER OF PERSPECTIVE

"Philosophers are in the right when they tell us, that nothing is great or little otherwise than by comparison."

Jonathan Swift

Gulliver's Travels

Prompt

Write a story about a 'scoffing son.'

He lay down his burden and sensed the air. It was hot. The trail was cold. He was tired. The path ahead of him was infinite. Madness had brought him out this far from civilization. Madness would lead him home again. He thought of the others who would be waiting. He thought how impressed they would be that he had travelled so far to retrieve such a prize.

He picked up his load and plodded on. The sun was merciless. So he thought of the coolness of his home. The glare was relentless. So he thought of the still darkness that would welcome him when he finally arrived.

Shadows began to dart to and fro overhead. At first he thought there would be relief from the sun, but that did not happen. Each time the sun reappeared brighter than ever. It seemed to tease him. So he redoubled his efforts and with renewed strength pushed forward. He would be the victor.

His thoughts alone kept him going. Cool thoughts. Triumphant thoughts. He would come to the threshold and pass through it with his prize held high. The farther he entered, the greater the relief from the blazing heat of day. He would once again feel the cool depths of home. He would welcome the musty smell of thick earthen walls protecting him from the sun's taunts. At last he would see all the others. They would gather and marvel that he had braved both distance and tortuous heat to bring home food this glorious: a delicacy that no one had ever tasted before.

The sun did not care about his imaginations. It considered his thoughts impudent, so it burnt hotter and brighter and more furious than ever. He now began to feel moisture leeching from his aching body. His steps became slower and less sure. His burden weighed heavier and heavier upon him. Thoughts of home began to recede. The sun could see his hopelessness. The sun! He was certain it was rejoicing at his misery.

He was lost now. Heat induced disorientation had misdirected him. He lay his burden down in hopes of sensing how far off he had gotten from the path. The sun had burnt out of him all his instinctive knowledge of direction. Panic set in. He walked this way and that way. He forgot what he was doing. Round and round in circles he went. All the while the sun smiled mockingly.

***

"Ee- ew! What's that?" The little girl jumped back from the blob that lay on the sidewalk.

Her companion stepped up bravely and poked it with a stick.

"It's only a big ant." He said. "Stupid ant. Looks like it was trying to carry that huge piece of candy."

"The boy scooped up the semi melted mess and offered it to the girl. "Want some?"

"Yuk. No thanks."

CHAPTER FOUR

A FORTUNATE MISFORTUNE

"Serendipity is the kinder sister of Accident."

Alexa Anne Kempson

Prompt

Write a story about resignation using a ski lodge as a setting. Include a widower and have a wallet figure prominently in the story.

Up until yesterday everybody who knew of Jack Martin thought him to be the luckiest man alive. The same thought could be applied to him today – well, sort of. It all started twenty four hours ago.

A swarm of Paparazzi greeted the couple as they checked into Montclaire Ski Lodge. This particular scenario had been repeated innumerable times since Jack and Lacey had married seven weeks ago. Served him right for marrying the world's top fashion model. Oh well, it was a punishment he could live with. How a poor, boring accountant had managed to take Lacey Vanhelm, model and heiress, off the bachelorette shelf, no one could figure out, including Jack. He wasn't bad looking, but he was no movie star. Hardly an heir to a fortune, Jack had been adopted at birth by a blue collar couple from Passaic, New Jersey. He was pretty much shunted aside in most photo ops and interviews anyway, so he easily melted into the background. Being the Invisible Man suited him fine. Jack just kept thanking his lucky stars that he had let go of his skinflint ways long enough to buy that package deal to St. Thomas where Lacey had been on a shoot. However it had happened, the media loved it. She was 'riches to more riches' and he was 'rags to riches.' What more could the public want?

The couple managed to escape to their suite in record time. Jack was glad the initial hoopla was over. He knew that the resort management had rounded up the photographers and sent them packing. That meant some 'kick off your shoes time' in the room with Lacey, or so he thought. Lacey decided that they might as well get some skiing in since the Paparazzi were gone and that wouldn't last. So they suited and goggled up, bribed her security guards to look the other way, grabbed some skis and headed off to try their hand at the killer slope.

It was great just being faceless skiers in a crowd. Up the lift and swooshing down the slope, racing and taking minor risks made for a refreshing afternoon. They were just about to return to the lodge and submit themselves to the ranting of her irate manager when it happened. Lacey had lagged behind a bit to deal with some cantankerous equipment. From out of nowhere a snowmobile came flying down the slope and slammed into Jack. The hapless accountant was sent hurtling into a tree. He bounced off and began a very slow roll down the slope gathering snow as he went until the human snowball disappeared over a cliff. A horrified Lacey stood watching helplessly as her husband careened out of sight into the abyss. Then she passed out. Unfortunately, her head managed full contact with a sharp rock, and that was it for Lacey Vanhelm, top model and heiress.

Joey Carrelli, petty criminal, swung out of the stolen snowmobile and looked around. No one else had witnessed the mayhem. He walked quickly over to Lacey. Whoever she was, she was dead for sure. His initial panic soon gave way to a plan. Joey always had a plan. They were never very good plans, but Joey seldom realized that, until he found himself running from the law. He reasoned that 'Snowball Man' wouldn't be found until spring, if ever. All he had to do was put Sleeping Beauty into the snowmobile and take her back to the Lodge saying that he had seen her get hit. He saw the driver jump out and take off. She was barely alive, so Joey heroically rushed her back for help. That sounded good. He figured he might get something out of it. At any rate he would disappear pretty quickly.

Joey arrived carrying Sleeping Beauty into the Lodge. A feeling of panic swept over him when he saw the lobby filled with police and photographers. The irate manager had summoned the police and the photographers crawled in after them. When the photographers saw Joey cameras started clicking right and left. One cop relieved him of his burden and another grabbed his arm. Next thing Joey knew he was in the swankiest room he had ever seen in his life being told that his wife was dead. Why did they think Sleeping Beauty was his wife? A silent and dumfounded Joey Carrelli sat there trying to figure out a way to escape. He kept hearing the words whispered around him: "He's in shock." Was he ever!

The doctor looked him over and pronounced him undamaged, but gave him something to help him sleep. The doc suggested the cops interview him tomorrow. Right now he needed to rest. All Joey could think of was getting out and and getting out fast. All he ended up doing was falling asleep for about a million hours.

He jerked awake around 7 AM when he heard someone enter the adjoining room. Tossing on a robe he was greeted by a hot breakfast and a newspaper. A good breakfast would help him come up with another plan.

He picked up the newspaper and almost choked on his croissant. A huge headline read: "Top Model Lacey Vanhelm Killed in Snowmobile Accident." Beneath it was a photo of the model. It was Sleeping Beauty all right. Joey read all about the heiress and her husband – how they had snuck out for a day on the slopes only to have it end in tragedy; how the bereaved husband was unavailable for interviews until he had spoken to the police. The police! That's when it hit Joey: he had killed a famous model and her husband and now the police were on their way to get his story. He was a goner for sure.

Joey grabbed some clothes he found in a suitcase. They fit like a charm. The nice thing was that he found a wallet – a fat one. He opened it and got the shock of his life. There was this New Jersey driver's license in it and the face on it, staring at Joey, was his own. He sat down on the edge of the bed to ponder the meaning of the fat wallet with his picture in it. He lived in New York, not New Jersey. He didn't drive – at least not legally. After a long time deep in meditation, he realized what it must mean. He had been born in New Jersey. He had been adopted. He had had a twin. They were separated at birth. Lacey Vanhelm's husband, Jack Martin, must be his long lost twin.

Nothing like this had ever happened to Joey in his entire life. It was his big break. For all that anybody else knew he was Lacey's husband. That meant he was rich, really rich. Joey let that sink in a while. He had a choice. He could run like a rabbit and vanish before they found the 'Snowball Man' or he could resign himself to his new fate. Joey knew he wasn't the brightest light bulb or he would have been a more successful criminal. But he wasn't that dumb. Jack Martin pocketed his wallet and waited for the police to arrive.

CHAPTER FIVE

REALLY, REALLY LOST

"So now all who had escaped death in battle or by shipwreck had got safely home except Odysseus…"

Homer

The Odyssey

Prompt

Think of a memorable character (from a book, film or TV show). Craft a story about the character losing the most valuable thing he or she owns.

25

The young woman had never run harder in her entire life. No wonder! This time she actually was running for her life along with her friends. Should she and her companions be caught...? She blocked the thought from her mind. She never ought to have come here it in the first place. Look where her rashness had landed her. Her former life seemed far away, unreal. At least it had prepared her in one aspect: she could run.

They had reached the woods. The trees ought to provide some cover for them. They all stopped to catch their breath. Her sense of security was a false one and short lived. Out of nowhere their enemies descended upon them. One by one she saw her comrades fall victim to the army. Then they were all spirited away to the dark fortress.

Once there, face to face with her nemesis and surrounded by the army of evil soldiers who had brought them, she huddled with her band of companions. She was afraid, but drew strength from her friends. Each one, so different from the other, offered her a unique kind of comfort. Her little group was utterly powerless in the face of evil, but they refused to give in to the demand made of them. At last their adversary began the torture that would lead to an agonizing end for her dearest friend. It was sure to be repeated, although differently for each of them, but the result would be the same: death.

She acted quickly, almost without thinking, in order to save her friend. Her efforts met with success and had the unexpected consequence of killing their tormentor. Unfortunately, as she looked around, she realized that her effort had only postponed the inevitable. So she and her companions prepared themselves for certain death at the hands of the soldiers. Unbelievably, instead of death, they were handed their freedom. The quartet returned as quickly as possible to the place where their quest had begun.

Their taskmaster who had sent them upon their dangerous adventure now became their benefactor. Each of her friends received his long sought for, and well deserved, reward. Their journey had brought them all that they had hoped for. She shared her friends' joy as their expectations came to fruition. Now she looked to him for her desire to be fulfilled. What bitter disappointment she tasted when she learned that all the gifts had been given out. There was nothing left for her. Her would-be benefactor departed leaving her hopes dashed.

All seemed lost when another appeared, as if by magic, and gave her what she needed. Words. She had only needed words; she possessed everything else. The young heroine stepped up expectantly, until she looked down. Alas! In the preceding fracas with her enemies Dorothy had lost one of her ruby slippers. She had one shoe too few to return to Kansas.

CHAPTER SIX

WHERE HE SAT

"Our favorite memories are often ones that never really happened."

Alexa Anne Kempson

Prompt

Write about an object of significance from your youth.

I ran my hand across the couch. The upholstery was fine linen, though old and worn now. Even so, there was enough nap that it pilled here and there making patches rough to the touch. The couch had once been my mother's pride and joy. In the 60's 'Avocado' had been the color to have. I smiled to myself at the thought of that design *faux pas*. Turbid green does not endear an object to anyone. Yet, Mother had spared no expense to make this sofa the centerpiece of her living room. The cost was a sacrifice she gladly made for her two girls. We needed a proper sitting parlor for courting.

I smiled at the thought of her old fashioned ideas that never quite synchronized with the 'Mod' era. To her the Beatles were four nice looking boys with hair much too long, and the Beach Boys needed to quit surfing and get real jobs. Now, as an adult, I realized that many of her observations were tongue in cheek, but as a teenager they had aggravated me no end.

I sat on the end of the cushion in a deep well, one carved by years of bottoms preferring to sit by the table that had the lamp on it. We read or listened to the record player or just watched the back yard through the huge picture window. It was a peaceful corner, a thinking spot, a safe place. It never saw excitement, or even courting, despite Mother's hopes, but there was one time that this nook, this sanctuary, saw both, at least to my mind.

I was an awkward, acne prone and smart girl – the trifecta of unpopularity for a junior high schooler. The first day at my new school I sat at the end of a long table in the tomb-like lunchroom and nervously awaited the homeroom bell. I kept to myself. I had left the uniform security of my elementary school for this unknown country of changing classes and a variety of teachers. Worst of all, I had lost many of my friends, the rich ones, who were enjoying the luxuries of various private schools.

I sat there not daring to look around. I knew that a boy sat next to me. I refused to risk humiliation by looking his way, much less engaging in a conversation. As I sat with my head down pretending to read a book, a piece of paper from the Boy's direction was shoved under my nose. I panicked imagining the tormenting words it probably contained. "Have you been beaten by an ugly stick?" Fatty, fatty, two by four can't get through the bathroom door." "How did you get those craters, moon-face?" Instead

29

what I saw was a proposed game of hangman. Without looking at the Boy I wrote the letter 'e' and passed it back. He countered by drawing the base of the gallows. My guess of an 'i' was similarly met, and the post of the gallows went up. Back and forth it went until I was outwitted by the hangman over the word 'jury.' The last thing I read before the bell rang was: "Hi, I'm Jack Brown. What's your name?" Hesitantly I scribbled, "My name is Annie Fletcher."

The bell rang. I still had not faced my hangman. When I did, my eyes were met with the handsomest boy I had ever seen. He wore a broad smile and held out his hand for me to shake. I did. We parted, I for my part, in shock that he had not once flinched even after seeing my face. I was in love.

We were both in many of the same advanced classes throughout junior high. Each morning before school I sat on my Avocado sofa. Like a race horse chomping at the bit and pawing to get out of the gate, I eagerly awaited 7:20 AM so I could race to the bus stop. School meant seeing Jack, and seeing Jack meant happiness.

Our friendship grew over the three years. It was never a boy-girl thing. It was more of a counselor – patient thing. He sought my advice about girls in general and about whomever he was dating at the time, in particular. By ninth grade he was in need of a calculus tutor, and that task fell naturally to me. I welcomed any opportunity to spend time with Jack. We met on Tuesday afternoons after school in one of the classrooms. One glorious Tuesday afternoon the school was shut down for fumigation. That day Jack came to my house.

Mother was using the kitchen table to cut out a dress and so that left only the living room for us to study in. After charming my mother, as he charmed anyone of the female sex, Jack plopped down on the Avocado sofa next to the table with the lamp. We waded through half our lesson, when suddenly, spotting the record player, he bolted up and put on the Monkees 'Last Train to Clarksville.' Then he did the most extraordinary thing. He grabbed my hand and whirled me into a frenzied dance. Mother came rushing in to see all the commotion and was sucked into the vortex of rock and roll music. We danced, we laughed and danced some more.

30

TWISTS

The rapturous afternoon ended all too soon. Mrs. Brown's honking car horn sounded loudly in front of our house. Jack gathered his books, bade us goodbye and closed the door upon the most wonderful day of my life. I sat down upon the Avocado sofa and stroked the scratchy linen.

The years passed and Jack and I married – other people, of course. Each high school reunion we would meet as old school chums and swap family stories. He never suspected how I felt all those years ago. Then one reunion he wasn't there. Cancer had taken him.

Now mother had passed. Lindsey and I sorted, divided and tossed away a lifetime of her possessions. Exhausted I collapsed onto the frayed and faded sofa.

"I'll call Goodwill to come get that old thing It's too ratty for me." Lindsey said.

I ran my hand over the spot where he sat and replied.

"That won't be necessary."

.

CHAPTER SEVEN

SWEETIE PIE

"A rose by any other name would smell as sweet."

William Shakespeare

Romeo and Juliet

Prompt
Use these words to write your story: dog trainer, bills, beach, pie.

Looney Lucy was out walking with her dog. Dog walking is not an unusual activity. On any given day big dogs, small dogs, old and young, can be seen straining at their leashes while they mentally curse their owners for being so pitifully slow. Lucy's pet happened to be walking his mistress on the beach. In fact, he walked her on the beach every day at exactly the same time. At precisely 8 am, 365 days a year, rain or shine, Gaugin and Lucy could be seen taking their first step off the boardwalk onto the beach. Normally there's not anything unusual about the sight of an old lady walking her dog on the beach, but Looney Lucy and Gaugin were the proverbial exception.

Gaugin was always clad in a tam, boots, a plaid cape and what Lucy referred to as "dog trainers" more commonly called doggie diapers. Lucy was well known to the beach goers and most gave her a wide berth, understandably so. Like her dog she dressed rather oddly, always resembling a hippie, but from the 1930s. Nothing was static about her. Miscellaneous pieces of her clothing were continually tossed up here and there by the boisterous ocean winds. Her hair was as free as her drapery and whipped around her head rather wildly. The pair had the appearance of a witch with her familiar, which in this case, happened to be a Schnauzer in diapers instead of a black cat. Sometimes she would pause and face the water, lift her hands and speak. Whether she addressed herself or God, Poseidon or the water, no one knew. No one asked.

I walk the same beach though not as faithfully as Lucy and Gaugin, but when I do I always stop and chat with the pair of them. The first day we met I was preoccupied with my recent loss, if you can call it that. What do you call it when you return from Afghanistan and find out that your fiancé has run off with your father – a two for one loss? I looked up and saw Looney Lucy and her dog approaching, she in floaty garments and he in natty attire and diapers. We passed each other; then Lucy turned around and shouted to me: "No one is allowed to look so mournful on this beach. It upsets Gaugin." I couldn't resist. I turned back and that is how we struck up our odd friendship. The minimum requirement was that I address Gaugin politely at our encounters.

I poured out my woes to her as we strolled along, although I am not normally a guy that does that sort of thing. The sun reflecting off the azure water, the white sands, warm and soft beneath my feet, the smell of salt – beach things – all conspired to loosen my tongue. Lucy was the better listener of the two. Gaugin was easily distracted by just about everything. He chased waves in the surf. He bolted at seagulls with fish in their bills. He darted after sand crabs. But Lucy stood still by the water, nodding sympathetically and saying nothing, which was all I needed.

Day by day I grew to think of her, no longer as Looney Lucy, but just Lucy. We had met most mornings for several months when she began to speak about herself. I realized I had monopolized our outings and knew little of her life. So I stood still by the ocean listening while Lucy poured out her words and Gaugin romped amid the surf. She still lived in her childhood home. She read only books written prior to 1955. Until retirement she had worked at a bank for fifty years – in the same location. She called it 'the institution.' The bank itself had mutated through five name changes and the building, three renovations, making Lucy the real institution. She had never married and had no children. Her only family consisted of a beloved great-niece.

Then one day Lucy and Gaugin didn't show up. This one absence made it the worst day of my life. Not war or losing a fiancé and father seemed as horrible. For the next month I came each day and was disappointed. One day I courageously resolved to read the obituaries in the collection of old newspapers that cluttered my living room, but not finding her name was somewhat comforted. The next day when she appeared it was sans Gaugin. She quietly explained that he had passed and she had been in mourning. For several days we walked side by side silently listening to other conversations around us: the waves whooshing to the birds, the birds chattering to the wind and the wind whispering softly to the waves.

Eventually we spoke again. It seems there was one bright spot in her life. She had filled the void of Gaugin's loss with a new companion lately arrived and welcomed into her house. Her name was "Sweetie Pie." Judging by her absence, this new pet, I supposed, was not a beach walker. It didn't seem to bother Lucy, though. Her praise of Sweetie Pie was exalted to the Heavens. On and on she went about how adorable she was, how attentive and comforting. Lucy was sure I would love little Sweetie Pie. Sweetie Pie would be just the thing to perk me up. She had a way of bringing joy to all. She was young and sprightly and just seeing her made you feel alive. I assumed I was being invited to Lucy's house to meet the beach-shy canine, but an invitation never came.

After a few weeks I began to fear that Lucy was dying and was intended to leave me the dog in her will. One day she said that I was going to meet Sweetie Pie that very morning. Not long after this remark Lucy stopped and pointed. I looked up and saw what can only be described as Aphrodite rising from the sea foam. The goddess headed straight for us.

"Hi. I'm Grace, Lucy's great-niece. I'll be staying with her for a while. She's told me all about you. I'm looking forward to getting to know you."

Sweetie Pie was definitely not a dog.

CHAPTER EIGHT

WINDS OF CHANGE

"A surprise is something that happens when you are looking for something else."

Alexa Anne Kempson

Prompt

Write about Valentine's Day without mentioning these words: Valentine's Day, cupid, love, roses, flowers, hearts or February.

TWISTS

Whisking around the corner as fast as I could I was hit in the face with one of those wintery Chicago winds that sucks all warmth from you. I lowered my head and plowed forward into the gale. High winds were nothing. I was going to make it to the coffee shop on time. Three years of working in the Windy City had meant one thing only: today at precisely 6 PM I was to reunite with my other half.

We had been banned from the joy associated with the very day when embracing exceeds every other form of human interaction. For us there was no physical encounter, no 'til death do us part.' Before we parted we embraced, instead, an idea. We promised to meet when the gathering fury was all was over, on this date, that special day which begets the union of minds and of souls and of bodies. We would become one forever. And so we were bereft of each other, parted by circumstance and miles that could not be traversed. Letters, cold substitutes for the warmth of presence, were all that had passed between us.

A few blocks worth of memories of our meeting raced through my mind as I hastened to my destination. Boring classes designed to engender sleep were made tolerable only by riotous notes passed to me from an unknown donor sitting behind me. Four months of trying to discover the note-giver, and another month of working up the nerve to reply. Then all wonder broke loose. We discovered that there is such a thing as a soul mate. We both came to life: late nights eating impossibly unhealthy food, chain smoking, studying and playing. Days we silently wove our paths to encounter each other as we maneuvered our class schedules. There were romantic rendezvous: rare, expensive dinners at fancy restaurants; more frequent cheap meals at diners. Snowball fights and movies; laughing and crying; dancing and singing; sainting and sinning. All of it together.

What should have grown onward and upward until no higher ecstasy could be attained was wickedly interrupted. War. It hurts and divides and kills. But we refused to listen to its voice. A cruel December day had shaken the nation. Our own private world was made all the more bitter in January when he received his summons. The following month we parted mid-month on the very day whose celebration defies war's dark philosophy of hate.

37

We steeled ourselves against separation by firmly knitting our souls together. We were determined that nothing could sever their divine communion. War came and overshadowed the world, but my soul never darkened, not once. In the very ether above me our souls mingled and communed. I counted the days until we would be reunited. War's end came in all but the formality of a treaty.

At the coffee shop I battled the door, the wind countering my every effort. A young soldier seated nearby leapt up and conquered the dragon of a door. I politely thanked him and, in doing so, beheld eyes that momentarily held me in such a grip, I could barely escape. Joyful pools of blue into whose gentle depths I felt I was falling. Tearing myself away, I searched the tables in the crowded cafe. Nowhere was my soulmate to be seen. Nowhere was there a place to sit. Again the gentle eyes met mine, this time inviting me to sit at their table.

I thanked them and sat. The kind eyes ordered me some coffee. Instinctively they knew I was waiting for someone else. They politely offered to sit at the counter so my 'expected one' could sit with me. Not yet. I would wait until he came. I would introduce him to the gallant knight who had opened the door. I breathlessly poured out my story to the listening eyes. As I spoke, the joyful eyes became concerned. I exhaled the finale of my tale and fell quiet. The eyes became shy and looked away, then down at the table for a long time. Finally, they lifted and trapped me once more. Grave eyes asked my soul mate's name. When they heard, they darkened in despair – sad glistening pools brimming over. My soul mate, my other half, the sorrowful eyes had known well and had watched die last month in Ardennes: the Battle of the Bulge.

It could not be. I had not felt death in my soul. I would have known if half of me had died. I wept. A warm hand reached out and held mine, cold and small. He has never let go of it these past sixty-five years.

CHAPTER NINE

THE NAY-SER

"Yeah, there's a lot of bad 'isms' floatin' around this world, but one of the worst is commercialism. Make a buck, make a buck."

Alfred, the Macy's Janitor

Miracle on 34th Street

Prompt

Think of a product you would never use. It is about to be taken off the market. Write a letter to the manufacturers convincing them not to remove it.

39

THE PRODUCT

The 'Nay-ser' Hair Removal Tool by Hairaway Products.

Tired of hairs protruding from your nose? Try the Nay-ser! Tiny, focused laser beams remove hair permanently. Easy to use, permanent results. Useful for ear hair, too!

***

THE LETTER

Hairaway Products
555 75th St.
New York City, NY 10031

Dear CEO of Hairaway Products,

I have recently been made aware that Hairaway Products is planning to remove the Nay-ser Nose Hair Removal Tool from the market. It is my understanding that there is no intrinsic problem with the Nay-ser, nor sanctions placed upon it by the government. It is ultimately a case that the Nay-ser is currently underperforming and its profits have fallen.

I must protest your course of action for several reasons, notwithstanding your desire to maximize your profits. First, let me remind you that in the past the Nay-ser's performance has been exemplary. Simply because there has been a temporary dip in the market share is an injudicious reason to scrap this fine product forever. Second, you hold patents on numerous products that must provide you with high profit margins. The revenue from appealing and broad-based merchandise is such that you ought to be able to offer a product with a limited market share (such as the Nay-ser), as long its generated revenue is within acceptable parameters. I believe that it is. Third, such a market is comprised of people – people who desperately need the benefits offered by your product.

This brings me to a personal appeal, namely, that I am one such person who depends on the Nay-ser. As an eighty year old man I may be considered over the hill by the general public, but to the ladies in my nursing home I am a stud muffin. I can regularly pick up the chick of my choice (often years younger than I) because of my fit physique and good looks. A part of my ability to outstrip the other male residents is that I easily eliminate the overgrowth of my nasal (and ear) hair by the use of the Nay-ser. Most of the men here find the process of plucking so painful that they rely on scissors to control their straggly offending hairs. The stubble produced by scissors cannot compare to the results of the Nay-ser: the painless and complete removal of hairs down to the pores.

No doubt you are in the prime of life and so are smirking at my proposal. Therefore, I need only remind you of this: you are not getting any younger and may one day find yourselves in need of the Nay-ser in order to fulfill your sexual desires. Therefore, I entreat you to reflect on my petition to reconsider suspending the production of the Nay-ser. Who knows, one day you may be in my shoes or in my nursing home.

Sincerely,
Methuselah Cratchett
Second Chance Nursing Home
123 Paradise Lane
Lost Cause, NV 89513

***

THE REPLY

ALEXA ANNE KEMPSON

Dad,

Even if we ditch the product, I've already told you a million times that I can get you all the Nay-sers you'll ever need.

Your Loving Son,
Lamech Cratchett
CEO Hairaway Products

PS. See you Sunday

CHAPTER TEN

THE TIN BOX

"Keepsakes are objects whose value is measured in love, not gold."

Alexa Anne Kempson

Prompt

Write about a keepsake.

43

Of all the places of interest in my house when I was growing up, I liked my parents' room best. It wasn't so much because of the small dresser in my dad's closet where he kept his candy bar stash. It wasn't my mom's cool short wave radio next to her bed that she used to listen to Radio Free Cuba every night.

Although Dad's nightstand with its stash of Mickey Spillanes, 007s and the ever present pack of cigarettes was pretty alluring, that isn't what drew me there. Nor was it the loose change Dad kept on the dresser. Although, from time to time, I lined my pockets with quarters that somehow accidentally fell off the dresser when I was nearby.

Not even Mom's perfumes that dotted her side of the dresser were the big draw. To most little girls it might have been her jewelry: her grandmother's ruby ring, the green tourmaline necklace, the high prong diamond ring and other delights.

It was none of these things. It was an old tin box that Mom kept in her drawer. I loved to sneak into the room and open the drawer where she kept it. It was shaped in a half moon with a hinged top that was fluted all around. Whatever the original design painted on it was, no one could tell now. Most of the paint was gone and the tin surface that remained was scuffed and pitted. But what treasures it held!

A half dozen broken chains of gold and silver lay intertwined on the bottom and, like a bird's nest, cradled precious things. There were various broken pieces of jewelry: rings with the stones fallen out; out-of-fashion items like sweater clips and collar pins; silver ornaments bent out of all recognition. There were odd shaped pieces of jewelry whose purpose defied my imagination, no matter how I strained it. There were loose glass beads of every color – a rainbow of neglected spheres rolling around as if looking for their lost mates.

Snips of paper were there too. Old receipts jumbled with illegible notes and post cards. There was a torn photo of a younger mother as queen of the Harlequin Ball. I remember fingering one fragile ribbon that couldn't have served any useful purpose that I could divine. But it was there, purposely kept by my Mom, for reasons known only to her. It must have been important.

Therein lies the mystery of the tin box. It wasn't that it was filled with valuables that any thief might seek. It was filled with treasures, treasures that are of importance only to the one who is initiate to their value. For some reason my mother intentionally kept those things. Each had a story to which I was not privy. Perhaps these seemingly worthless things spoke more clearly of who she was than the fine jewelry, her position as a wife and mother, her career as a teacher. I suspect that if these objects had a translator they would speak the depths of my mother's soul more clearly than any other voice.

Round and round we went, my three siblings and I. My mother had died and we had piled her seemingly insignificant possessions in our midst. Most of her valuables she had designated already and only the small, the least noteworthy things remained. Beginning with my brother, the eldest, we took our turns choosing the items we wanted. I bit my lip as first my older brother, then my older sister made their selections. After each chose, I breathed a sigh of relief. When my turn came I snatched up the tin box as though it were the Holy Grail. Now the tin box stays by bed and each night whispers my mother's goodnight to me.

CHAPTER ELEVEN

SURPRISE

"O matre pulchra filia pulchrior"

Horace

Odes

Prompt

Write a story about fatherhood, with a florist as the main character and a new dress as the key object. Set your story in a restaurant.

Martin nervously tidied up the silverware on the table, not that it needed tidying. He was self-conscious. Never in his sixty-two years would he have guessed that he would resort to a dating agency, an online one to boot. But he did. Now he was waiting for Priscilla Folger. Her name alone made him nervous. No one was named Priscilla these days and her last name was a brand of coffee. She said that she was a fun-loving, divorced middle age woman of forty-five. He was pretty sure that was a lie. What woman gives her real age? She was probably sixty-five if she was a day.

At this point it didn't matter. Martin was lonely. How was he to know he was so boring that his wife had to take up with that hardware store owner? How could a man who dealt in cold, hard metal things be more exciting than a florist? Flower arrangement was an art. *Bradfords* was an institution. In Boston no Brahmin daughter wed, no patriarch or matriarch died, no politician rallied without flowers by *Bradfords*. That meant he rubbed elbows with the highest classes of society. They called him by his first name. That's pretty damn exciting, but apparently not to Gloria.

He looked up and caught the eye of a server on his way back to the kitchen. He ordered another scotch and soda. Why was she divorced? What was wrong with her? Online dating sites didn't offer much in the way of explanation. Her picture was decent, at least what was visible. Her face was fairly sexy for a middle aged woman. Maybe the photo was touched up? More likely it was twenty years old. He could just picture her in her new red dress that had 'flair,' the one she mentioned she'd be wearing tonight. It would probably be a size too small. She'd put on heavy makeup and spray her hair to death, all to avoid looking middle aged. When had he gotten middle aged? Boring and middle aged. Why would anyone want him? Gloria didn't.

His drink appeared before him. Thanking the waiter he slugged back half of it. Where was he? Oh, yeah. Gloria didn't want him, so why would a forty something divorcee? What had he written about himself? He was a successful businessman, loved reading, sailing and that he was fifty-four. Well, a little lie wouldn't hurt. After all, men keep their sex appeal long after women. He tossed back the rest of the drink and ordered another. His photo was taken around his fifty-fifth birthday, or was it his forty- fifth? No matter. He looked young for his age and worked out five or six times a week. She'd be lucky if he was interested in her.

Priscilla said she was an artist and owned a small gallery. That probably meant she was strange, but called it free spirited. But he was free spirited, too, by damn and not the least bit boring. He polished off his third drink and was feeling more confident. When Gloria left him he moved from disbelief to anger to looking for someone fairly quickly. The problem was that he knew most of the age appropriate women in town, married and unmarried. Not one of them was looking at him. That about sums up why he was here. He laughed to himself. Maybe Priscilla was pulling out all the stops for tonight, only to be bitterly disappointed.

He was about to order a fourth glass of courage when he noticed an attractive woman looking around the restaurant. She was tall and slim, but not skaggy looking. She had a very intelligent face. He guessed she was closer to forty than fifty. Suddenly Martin grew uncomfortable. She had on a red dress with 'flair,' alright, and looked mighty good in it. It was obvious that she was looking for him, Martin Bradford, but probably expecting a much younger Martin Bradford. He cursed himself for fudging his age and photo. He half-stood to acknowledge her entrance.

She caught his eye and smiled a big warm, friendly smile. It was too late to escape now. She wove her way gracefully, like a dancer, to his table. He invited her to sit, and before he could get a word out, she waved off a cocktail and began her questions. Yes, he was Martin Bradford. Yes, he grew up in Boston. Yes, he went to St. Bartholomew High School. Yes, he knew a Mary Callahan there. Did they date their senior year? Yes, for a time. The questions stopped as abruptly as they had begun. She looked straight at him, silent eyes boring into his. Familiar eyes… eyes from the past. He searched her face, then broke the silence, "You're my…"

"Daughter." she finished his sentence.

CHAPTER TWELVE

I'M OK – REALLY

"Semel emissum volat irrevocabile verbum."

("A word once released flies around never to return.")

Horace

Epistles

Prompt
Write a fictional scary encounter with your hairdresser/barber.

Monday mornings are never much fun at the office, but this particular Monday took the cake. I sat at my desk trying to accomplish something when Jana passed my cubby. I ignored her as best I could her as she lingered there staring at me, but there was no use in trying to prevent the inevitable. For the fifth time that day I smiled back at the face of a concerned coworker. No, I was not dying. I didn't have cancer. Yes, I was sure. I realize how it must look. Adjusting the multi-colored scarf wrapped around my denuded head, I launched one more time into the story of what actually had happened.

The last Saturday of the month was always my regular appointment at my hairdresser's. Chloe was part magician, part artist – at least with hair. Somehow she managed to take ten years off me and, at fifty- nine, I greatly appreciated that. She swore that as long as she lived, I would never be gray, develop a uni-brow or sport an old lady mustache. Needless to say, despite the difference in our ages, she was my best friend. So I was looking forward to this past Saturday.

When I arrived at Shear Sexy Salon I was simultaneously disappointed for myself and happy for Chloe. She had just left the salon in heavy labor. I was given the option of rescheduling or keeping my appointment with another technician, Liesel, who had arrived that day from Scandinavia. She had come highly recommended. So I opted for the latter and was ushered to her chair.

Liesel had long silky blond hair, was nine feet tall and built like a Victoria Secret model. I figured I had hit the jackpot for substitute hairdressers. She seated me and asked me in a heavy accent what I was there for today. I replied, 'the works.' She nodded energetically at me. So I settled in for a trim, color, eyebrow wax and eyelash dye job.

After 8 years Chloe knew all my sensitivities. Liesel had known me eight minutes and didn't, so I carefully laid them out for her. She smiled showing her snow white teeth and nodded – a lot. Conversation wasn't her forte, but I could use some peace and quiet. I closed my eyes and she went to work dabbing on the color on my roots.

After about ten minutes my scalp began to feel a little warm. I mentioned this to Liesel. Her eyes grew large and she nodded energetically, babbling something in what I assumed was Swedish or Norwegian. I figured this must be normal and, since it didn't really hurt, I it go. While the hair color was taking Liesel laid me back and applied the brow wax. The swish, swish of her ripping off the waxing strip was accompanied by a little more pain than usual, but Swedes, after all, were known for their aggressive massages so I assumed this was a typical Scandinavian cosmetician diva technique. Next I closed my eyes. On went the eyelash dye. Whoa! Now that hurt. In fact, my whole head felt like it was on fire.

Suddenly the salon manager rushed over to Liesel's station. She yelled at the Valkyrie: "Nyet! Nyet! " I was afraid to open my eyes fearing permanent blindness from the lash dye. Next thing I knew my head was being washed and sprayed with water for all its worth. All the while the salon manager kept interspersing "oh, my Gods" with "I really am terribly sorry for the mix-up."

Needless to say I was beyond curious. I was panicked despite the manager's reassurances. Her offer of a lifetime of free hair care scared me even more. As soon as she spun me around to face the mirror, her generous offer made sense. I was staring at a bald head and a face sans eyelashes and eyebrows.

During the five stunned minutes when I could neither move nor speak, she explained. Somehow there was confusion about Liesel. The salon had assumed she was Liesel Laarsen their new Swedish hair technician. This was not the case. Her name was Liesel Larinsky newly arrived from the Ukraine and looking for work as a receptionist.

I concluded my story for Jana. Her sympathetic stare alerted me that she had not believed a word I said. Gossip at the office had prejudiced her to a foreordained conclusion. She cooed that it was difficult to face reality, but she was sure I would in time. She handed me a card before walking away. I glanced at it: Enduring Compassion Hospice Care. I wasn't dying, but I did wonder if they had a good hairdresser there.

CHAPTER THIRTEEN

MY CUP RUNNETH OVER

"Blessed is he who expects nothing, for he shall never be disappointed."

Alexander Pope

Prompt

Write a story about an empty glass.

TWISTS

Nothing above,

Nothing below,

Side to side,

Head to toe,

Around and round,

And up and down,

Nowhere can my glass be found.

I set it somewhere to

Do some chore and

Now can't find it anymore.

It makes me mad since I am thirsty.

This situation is the worst be.

My throat is dry.

My tongue is thick.

My head is aching.

I'm feeling sick.

Barely standing

I squint and stare.

ALEXA ANNE KEMPSON

My longed for glass

Is on the stair.

I stagger over

And scoop it up.

Alas! It is

An empty cup

CHAPTER FOURTEEN

AMID GUERNICA

"But when he was still a great way off, his father saw him and had compassion, and ran and fell on his neck and kissed him."

Luke 15:20

Prompt

Write about a man looking for his son after a plane crash.

"Pennies from Heaven." "Autumn." "Fall." "Fallout." "The sky is falling." Useless words and phrases rushed through Jim's mind as he stared at the horrific scene around him. The chaos of distorted bodies and mangled wreckage all tumbled willy-nilly on the once golden Midwestern plain defied his ability to identify anything. It formed a surreal painting. "Guernica." "The Spanish Civil War." "Hemmingway." "A Farewell to Arms." Dr. Jim Frederickson quickly surveyed his own body. He had arms. And legs. Unlike so many around him, he was unharmed. "A Miracle." "Miracle on 34th Street." "Christmas." That was it. Kenny was born on Christmas. Oh God, where was Kenny?

He swiveled his head around and then began to wander aimlessly, looking now at a corpse and now at a seat cushion and now at some unrecognizable piece of machinery. The stench of burning flesh, grass and metal filled his nose. "Smell, scent, bloodhound, trail." To find Kenny he needed to follow a calculated trail. He had to retrace the trajectory of his path as he was ejected from the plane. His seat was near the back. When the plane had dropped without warning from the sky, Kenny had not been in the seat next to him. He couldn't remember why not. Most likely he was in the lavatory in the rear of the tail section.

Jim's eyes followed the huge gash hundreds of feet long that the plane had cut into the prairie. He located the tail section and headed for it. Far away the Rockies poked their heads above the flat horizon – mere grey pimples and not the purple mountain majesties of the song. Jim stopped. His medical knowledge told him that he was in shock, but he knew he had to focus or Kenny might be forever lost.   Beginning again he surveyed at least twenty feet either side of him of as he retraced his path. Many or all the passengers had been flung from the fuselage. He tried to avoid getting caught up by the pathetic sight of the injured and dead. Some of the living, like him, stood or wandered dazed and staring at the ground. He had no time to come to their aid.

The sounds of screaming and moans that had assaulted his ears as his journeyed back to the main wreckage began to taper off now. God have mercy. He was not insensible to the agonies of the helpless victims, but he had to find Kenny. "God, please, let none of these bodies be my son." His heart stopped when he saw the body of a young man on the ground not far from him. He approached cautiously, praying over and over that it not be Kenny.

His mind flashed back to when Kenny was three. Even then it was obvious that Kenny was special, a genius, a wunderkind. Jim was teaching him to catch a ball. "Put your hands together and watch the ball as I toss it. It will arc then drop. Estimate the trajectory and place your hands appropriately." The ball fell to the ground for the twentieth time and tears welled up in the tot's eyes. Jim had sharply called out to his son. "It's a sphere, Kenny…I've taught you about the properties of a sphere. I've taught you about motion." Once again he explained as precisely as possible the physics behind the path of a tossed ball so that his son could understand. He was annoyed that the child had made no progress at all. Kenny had just cried. "I can't catch it, Daddy." It had always been like that: Jim having exalted expectations of his son and his son having childish inclinations. Their relationship had only soured as Kenny grew older. With no mother in the picture to warm the father's scientifically calculated love, Kenny had walked out right after high school, but Jim knew that it was only temporary. Remorse swept over Jim. He wished their reunion had been sooner. So many years had been wasted. This trip, then the crash. Jim stopped and looked down at the body. Relief. It wasn't his son's.

A new sound that had long been competing with the death cries of the victims now became clear: sirens. Jim stood and looked. Police, firefighters and EMTs were at the perimeter of the scene. How long they had been there Jim didn't know. He abandoned his search for his son and ran towards them as if pushed by some invisible hand. He came to a young EMT bent over a body. The young man's voice was familiar, but it couldn't be. Kenny had been on the plane, hadn't he?

"Oh, Jesus! It's my father. He's dead." A horrified and bewildered Kenny looked up at a firefighter who readied the blanket to cover the corpse.

The firefighter gently draped the blanket over the body. "I'm sorry, Ken. What was he was doing on this plane anyway?"

"I have no idea. We haven't spoken in years."

CHAPTER FIFTEEN

MIDGE CAMPBELL

"And yet, believe me, good as well as ill,
Woman's at best a Contradiction still."

Alexander Pope

Of the Characters of Women
Epistle II: To a Lady

Prompt

Take out your high school yearbook & pick someone from your class. Write about what you think he or she is doing now. Go ahead & fictionalize that person.

Everyone liked her. You couldn't help it. It wasn't that Margaret Mary Campbell was pretty or athletic or exceptionally smart. Since she barely hit the five foot mark, 'Midget' was what we called her or 'Midge' for short, but she didn't mind. Weighing less than a St. Bernard, sporting huge thick glasses and hair like a Brillo Pad, Midge didn't seem likely to be admired. So why were we all drawn to her? Midge exuded what the rest of us teens at St. Ignatius High woefully lacked. The sisters called it virtue; the rest of us Ignatius inmates called it happiness or stupidity depending on the circumstances.

She always had a smile on her face. The teen angst that served as a constant tormenter to the rest of us fled Midge's miniature presence. She seldom suffered the frequent corporal punishment that many of us underwent; when she did, it left her more thoughtful than angry. We speculated that someday the Church would canonize her so we all fell to calling her St. Midge (behind her back, of course, and out of earshot of the sisters).

The lines for talking or consulting with Midge were longer than the confession lines on Saturdays. She was ever ready to assist in any capacity. Did you need something? Midge would screw her face up as though the mere fact of distorting her puckish features would make what you need magically appear. Even if she couldn't provide, she would offer the soundest advice you'd ever heard. It was liberally salted with whit. She had a ready ear for every problem. She never judged, never scolded, never left you feeling less than anything but well understood. Everyone from the captain of the football team to the school janitor claimed Midge as their confidant. I wouldn't have been surprised if Fr. Moynihan consulted her on occasion.

As I drove to my 50th reunion I wondered if Midge would show. She'd missed every one so far. It wasn't as if I were interested in her *that* way. I'd been happily married for thirty-nine years before Diane passed away and wasn't looking for a replacement. But at sixty-eight I understood that lust of the eyes prevailed when choosing a mate as a youth, but at my age there were other qualities to be preferred.

My thoughts drifted to the past fifty years of my life, and from there it was a hop, skip and a jump to fantasizing about Midge's life after high school. She didn't go to college: not enough brains or money. She'd wanted to do something special, something helpful to mankind. Of course! That was why we hadn't seen hide nor hair of her at past reunions. She joined the Holy Order of the Missionary Sisters of the Most Sacred Heart of Jesus and the Immaculate Heart of Mary, Reformed. Where did she go? I know. Africa. She always loved Africa. I could see her, a tiny figure working with a tribe of giant Watusis, but standing tall among them because of her inner spirit. They all loved her and probably called her after some tribal goddess or something. She had birthed their babies, cured their sick, comforted their mourners, and repelled their enemies single handed.

I surmised that it hadn't always been easy for her. I mean, it probably had been a tough haul for her to get to the Dark Continent. I bet she had hard time proving herself worthy of the Holy Order of the Missionary Sisters yada, yada,yada. I could see her sour faced Mother Superior, who being jealous of her angelic soul, assigned her the most insignificant and arduous duties. Midge, the Cinderella nun. Yeah. But she bore it with amazing patience. Of course that made Mother Superior all the more jealous. Nothing delighted the Abbess more than heaping cruel hardships on poor Midge hoping to break her and drive the saintly little person from the Abbey. But Midge's inspiration was St. Agatha. Agatha meant good and Midge was good. Besides, St. Agatha had a horrible suffering life and death. That suited Midge.

Her postulancy seemed endless. Then one day at breakfast Mother Superior choked on her Cheerios and died. Her replacement was very much into Vatican II reforms. Midge was fully professed right away and became Sister Agatha. Off came the old heavy black habits which made the old hag sisters furious, but the young sisters happy – and a lot cooler. But Midge, I mean Sister Agatha, missed her life of suffering. So she asked to be sent to Africa. There you have it.

I smiled to myself as I sauntered into the West Side Country Club. I picked up my name badge and looked over the others. My heart stopped when I saw one particular badge: Margaret Mary Campbell. She was coming. Everyone was as curious as I was. We all speculated about Midge. Two hours later we were rerunning nun stories from high school. I was in the middle of the one about Sister Kathryn Drexel who had gotten her habit hiked up in back, exposing her underwear when it happened. Midge arrived.

Every head turned, every face was in awe, every voice silenced. For in strolled Midge, all 4' 10" of her, her iron grey hair cropped short, swathed in leather head to toe, except for her arms which were bare and sported enough tattoos to inspire jealousy in any biker. Wait a minute. She was a biker and not just any biker. Little Margaret Mary Midget, Midge, St. Agatha Campbell was a Hells Angel.

CHAPTER SIXTEEN

GIANT FLIES INVADE NORWAY

"It is a far, far better thing that I do, than I have ever done; it is a far, far better rest that I go to than I have ever known."

Charles Dickens

A Tale of Two Cities

Prompt

Write a story with the headline 'Giant Flies Invade Norway.'

Ulv couldn't move, couldn't think, couldn't speak. If it is possible for a human being to cease being, but still exist, that is what Ulv felt like: a non-human being or a human non-being. A gentle tug on his shirt woke him from his stupor. He looked down at his twin sister Mirja kneeling on the floor next to his chair. Her blue eyes pleaded. "It is time."

Still Ulv did not move. But he did think. Six months ago when all the physicists had met in Oslo to brainstorm about solutions to the approaching disaster, his father had been among them. Ulv remembered his father upon his return, pale and ashen, his Norwegian complexion even whiter than usual. He didn't say a word to his two small children. He just hugged each of them with tear-filled eyes and strode to his lab.

Papa spent all his waking hours in his lab. There were few sleeping hours and they too were spent there. Ulv and Mirja took turns bringing him meals and fresh clothing. He never looked up when they entered, never acknowledged what they bore to him. His attention was completely fixed on the four monitors in front of him. To look at the various models that rotated and revolved on the multiple screens made Ulv's eyes hurt.

Three days ago the ten year old boy brought a tray of food to his father. As he entered he saw the last meal untouched. *"Spiser du, Papa."* The scientist neither moved, nor replied, but frantically worked the keyboard in front of him with his fingers. Ulv tiptoed out of the room to join Mirja in the den. As he shut the door behind him he took one last look at his father who had buried his shaggy, unkempt head in his hands and was weeping. That was the last time he saw his father alive.

"Det er pa tide." Mirja's eyes, deep blue like the fjord next to which their cabin nestled welled with tears. Her voice was pathetic. They had lost their mother before they ever knew her. All they had in the world was Papa. Now he was gone. What did it matter? His sister tugged gently again and handed him the newspaper. "Giant fluer invadere Norge." It was the code agreed upon by the physicists. When it appeared as a headline a scientist randomly selected was to initiate the protocol. It would either save or destroy the world.

Papa had been chosen to carry the burden of this mission. As his dying act Papa had left instructions to Ulv to carry out the orders. Now, it was time. How could Papa expect a ten year old boy to carry the fate of the world in his hands? It was too much.

He kissed Mirja and hugged her. Then he squared his shoulders and headed for the lab striding manfully and determinedly as he had seen his father do so many months before. He sat in his father's now vacated chair. He thought of his father lying at peace next to his mother. He thought of Mirja's fjord-blue eyes. He bowed his head then raised them to the monitors which flashed with colors and spirals and vortexes. He reached for the keyboard.

***

"Liam!" The boy's door flew open and the ten year old faced a very angry mother. "I called you ten minutes ago for dinner. Now turn off that computer and get downstairs. You can finish gaming after dinner and after your homework."

CHAPTER SEVENTEEN

SILENCE

"Sprecfien ist silbern, Schweigen ist golden."

(Speech is silvern, silence is golden.)

Attributed to a Swiss proverb

The Prompt

Weave a story around the mixed proverb "Silence is a Great Healer."

Many centuries ago there lay a village nestled among the hills in The Old Country. It was populated with devout and hardworking simple folk. There was nothing to take note of in this village. The women were not particularly beautiful, nor the men strong. The children were just children, plain and noisy.

So content were the people that troubles were few and far between. In the village there lived a Wise Man. On the rare occasions that difficulties did arise, since there was neither priest, nor judge, nor magistrate, the villagers brought their disputes to him. They also sought his advice about all manner of things: farming, husbandry, trading, cooking. There was no subject that eluded the wisdom of their village sage.

The village grew and prospered under the watchful eye of the Wise Man. Each day at dawn the men and women would tend to their work. The women busied themselves in the home and among the shops. Men trekked to the rich fields that lay beyond the village. But as it so often happens as wealth increased, dissatisfaction increased as well. All day the men grumbled of the long hours and harshness of their conditions. They blamed their neighbors or their wives. The women likewise performed their daily chores with increasingly sour faces and exclaimed that their husbands were lazy and their children worthless. Spouses, relatives, neighbors, even the very work that had brought them fulfillment and security, became the sources of their discontent. Men and women flocked to the village sage who began to be worn out from presiding over their petty complaints. Day and night they pestered him for quick judgments and easy solutions.

The villagers, who were of a hearty stock, began to fall ill. House after house was struck by a mysterious plague. The townsfolk began to fear for their lives. One day as the sun was just peeping over the horizon, the entire village, down to the nursing infant, came to the Wise Man and begged him to discover the cure for the plague that had fallen upon them. He dismissed them to their work, instructing them not to disturb him for three days. During those days the voice of the Wise Man could be heard above all the sounds of the village. He lamented and called out to God beseeching an answer for his people.

Just before dawn on the fourth day a terrible cry shattered the darkness. The people ran to the Wise Man's house. From the dark recesses he came forth and spoke to the assembled villagers.

"Silence is a Great Healer. Let your work, your play, your sorrow and joys be done without a word until I bear you different council."

He disappeared into the depths of his home and closed the door. The bewildered people stood for some minutes and then the sun rose. Each returned to his business in silence. Now only the sounds of villagers hard at work could be heard. They found that they could communicate in ways other than speaking. The effort was such that petty troubles yielded to the important things if life.

Soon all the sick recovered their health and returned to their routines. The village grew more prosperous than before. The Wise Man never reappeared to retract his words. After some months they sought him in his house but he was not there. Shrugging their shoulders they returned to their work in silence. Peace and prosperity again reigned in the little village.

***

I heard this story dozens of times as a child. Before bed I would curl up at my grandmother's feet next to our fireplace. Baba would tell stories of the Old Country. This was my favorite. "Molk, Molk! Silence, Silence!" Baba would say to me when I interrupted her or was too noisy at play. "Remember the silent village."

So it was natural that when I grew up I should want to visit the Old Country and all the villages, castles and vistas of which she spoke. I planned my trip with great care, marking on a map all the towns she mentioned in her stories. It was only long after her death, as I planned this trip, that I realized Baba had never given this village a name. It isn't that I thought the story was true, but there must be some quaint town that inspired the legend. Regretfully I dismissed the tale and the town from my thoughts.

I was in the middle of my travels having seen sweeping mountains with tiny villages stuffed into their crannies and expanses of colorful fields bearing crops alien to my knowledge when I began to think about my favorite story again. I had just finished with my third castle and was hopelessly lost in a remote area when I spotted a rough sign that read "Molk, 4 km." I rejoiced. This must be the town that the legend was based on. I threw my tiny vehicle into full throttle and sped down the bumpy road.

At the edge of town I slowed to pass leisurely down the main street. Stuccoed houses with thatched roofs and quaint shops with brightly painted signs flanked the road either side. Flower boxes exploded with color. Stone stoops, bleached by the sun, were swept clean. Mullioned windows with thick bubbled glass rippled with the reflected waning sunlight. A tall steeple topped with an iron cross loomed ahead at the end of the village street. Women with headscarves toted baskets while fat, rosy cheeked children gamboled around them. Occasionally an old stooped man sauntered past the women nodding his head in greeting. It was so incredibly charming that I decided to stay there, if there was such a thing as an inn. I knew that it meant rushing tomorrow to join a tour group, but I couldn't Baba down.

I found a hostel and greeted the innkeeper. In my best imitation of their language I asked for a room for the night. Pitying me and forgiving the butchering of his language he smiled and nodded, pushing the register towards me. I slept like a log that night.

The next morning I wandered around the village and chatted with the people as best I could. I was scheduled to meet the tour in the next town at noon, so I left far sooner than I wanted to. I raced to the castle, more accurately the castle ruins. After a long afternoon I found myself dining with our tour guide, a very nice woman whose ancestral roots were here. In fact, she had moved here from England five years ago after her retirement. She filled in the cracks on many of the sights I had seen on my visit. Baba would have been proud of me.

As we dined I mentioned my grandmother and that it was her stories which had brought me to see the Old Country. I laughingly gave her an abbreviated version of my favorite tale. I told her that I had stumbled upon a little village called Molk when I was meandering, lost in the countryside. I told her that I suspected the little village named itself after the legend rather than vice versa.

She brushed the crumbs from her mouth with her napkin and gave me a quizzical look. She asked why I thought that. I replied that the town and its people were so picture perfect I assumed it was for the benefit of tourists. She looked at me doubtfully and asked if they had spoken to me. I started to say yes, and then paused. I reflected on my visit and realized that I had spoken to them, but not one of them had said a word to me either in English or their language. I relayed this to my dinner companion. I posited that that the villagers' silence sustained the legend to amuse tourists like me. I will never forget her reply.

"Oh, no." She said as she folded her napkin and laid it in her lap. "It is a village of mutants. They are all born without vocal chords."

CHAPTER EIGHTEEN

A GIRL HAS TO MAKE A LIVING

There is a brotherhood of man
A benevolent brotherhood of man
A noble tie that binds all human hearts and minds
Into one brotherhood of man

Your lifelong membership is free
Keep a-giving each brother all you can
Oh, aren't you proud to be in that fraternity?
The great big brotherhood of man

Frank Loesser
How To Succeed in Business Without Really Trying

Prompt

Why would a Fortune 500 company start hiring fortune tellers?

Staring down the long table, every eye on me, everyone waiting with baited breath to hear what I had to say, I remembered where it began. There we all sat in a semi-dark room. We were a collection of women, oddly dressed – some, older; some, younger. We all had certain traits in common: big hair, scarves, bangly gold jewelry, heavy makeup, garishly painted nails and a deck of Tarot cards. It was a strategy room of sorts. Each participant had her own table and spent the day laying and reading cards. All the readings were recorded. Where they went or how they were used were things unknown to us fortune tellers. I smiled to myself recalling how I had come to be there among them.

I was in my parlor enjoying a cup of hibiscus tea when two men entered. They were dressed immaculately in Armani suits.

"Madame Delphi?"

"Yeeees." I looked up at two rigid faces devoid of expression.

"We are from Centrelle Biotronics." My ears pricked up. "This is Mark Henderson and I'm Kevin Hadley."

I began to lay my cards on the table without replying. I completed the first row, then, the second. I sat silently, my head spinning.

"Madame Delphi?"

We were all silent until I had finished laying another row of cards.

Circling a group with my index finger I looked up at the impassive faces. "You are here on beesiness."

A snort escaped Mark. He quickly swept his hand to his mouth in a disguised cough.

"You laugh at my accent. You think I am to be a stupid foreigner, a silly fortune teller."

His partner disavowed this and apologized. Both men eyed me carefully as I continued to plat with my cards the reason for their presence at Madame Delphi's. Row four went down.

72

Scrutinizing the newly laid rows, I again spoke. "Your beesiness is failing. Stocks have plummeted. Boom." I swept my hand towards the floor. "Profits (I rolled the 'r') are but a fraction of what you expected. Yeees?" This time Mark did not disguise the expression of his contempt.

I began to deposit the fifth row and paused midway. I carefully laid the next card and tapped it. "The head of your company is dead. Madme Delphi is wery, wery sorry."

"I bet." Mark's sarcastic comment merited another apology from Kevin.

"It was unfortunate. He couldn't deal with our situation and…" his voice trailed as he watched the remaining cards being deposited face down this time on the table.

I began to turn over each card of the last row. I stopped before the final two cards.

"You are in need of a new corporate head."

No sound from Mark, but this time it was Kevin who couldn't restrain himself He snapped impatiently.

"All this is information available to anyone who has read the newspapers about the problems that Centrelle has had the last six months."

"Yeeees, but did they divulge the name of the new CEO?"

"No, but our interim…"

"Phoo on your interim." I laughed. "Madame Delphi meant your permanent chief executive."

"We're still searching, though the current one may end up…"

"I spit on your search." I turned over the second to last card. "Ah! Madame Delphi knows who your new CEO will be. Yeeees. Yeeees. Madame Delphi knows who it will be." I caressed the last card, the revelatory card.

73

"Madame Delphi, that may be the case..." another snort from Mark warranted a threatening look from Kevin, "...but we are only here to request that you appear for an interview next Thursday at this address."

He handed me his business card.

"You will be reimbursed for any travel costs or other inconveniences. We simply ask that you tell us now whether or not you will come."

I slid the last card, which was still face down, towards me and raised it to my eyes. I stared at it for some moments. Without revealing it to the non-dynamic duo, I looked directly at them and replied. "Yeees, Madame Delphi will come."

And I had gone. I dutifully took my place among the other women. They did not have the advantage I had. Madame Delphi had the edge. Madame Delphi knew things they did not. Day after day, week after week my predictions succeeded where theirs failed. In a few months I, Madame Delphi, alone was left.

That was when I was brought in to meet the acting CEO. He was grateful to me for redirecting the company's fortunes. We shared a love for the world of psychic phenomena. He had utter faith in my gifts. I, too, was gratified. I saw to it that our relationship grew with the company's profits. We finally wed. As I honeymooned with my new husband, I thought about the two skeptics who had doubted my abilities. They would see.

The tragedy that struck was swift and final. I accompanied the body of my new husband back to Los Angeles. The funeral over, the will read, I met with the board of directors. How amusing it was to stride into the boardroom sans my Madame Delphi regalia. All the eyes in the room were on me and they had no idea who I was. Sleek in a suit from Rodeo Drive, I dropped my accent and introduced myself.

"Ladies and gentlemen, I am Delphine Panagakos. I hold an MB from the Wharton School of Business and a PhD from Harvard Business. You may remember me from my hobby as the fortune teller Madame Delphi. As you know over the last six months my late husband became the majority shareholder in Centrelle Biotronics. His will directed that the executive chair be turned over to me. So without further ado, let's get on with business.

Shooting a look directly at Mark and Kevin I winked the unmistakable message: "I told you so. Madame Delphi knew."

CHAPTER NINETEEN

AH, SPRING!

"Spring is nature's way of saying, "Let's party!""

Robin Williams

No prompt, just an old poem dredged up from High School. One morning as I got ready to go to Pensacola High I heard on the radio that the sun would cross the equator that day at 1:08 pm: thus the Vernal Equinox, the arrival of Spring. I dashed off this ditty. I made the mistake of showing it to a friend in one of my classes – during class. He snatched it from my hand, an event witnessed by the teacher who then invited my friend to read it to the class. Thank God for teachers who have a sense of humor.

TWISTS

At 1:08 pm today

The sun will turn its head this way.

In honor of this auspicious time

I have composed this little rhyme.

The 20th of March is here:

A time for joy, a time for cheer.

With a fifth of scotch and one of rum,

I'll celebrate that Spring has come.

When the 21st of March arrives,

I'll shade the sunlight from my eyes.

The chirping birds and springtime smell,

Can all drop dead and go to Hell.

CHAPTER TWENTY

THE DEERHORN PARTY

If you go down to the woods today
You're sure of a big surprise.
If you go down to the woods today
You'd better go in disguise!
For every bear that ever there was
Will gather there for certain,
Because today's the day the
Teddy Bears have their picnic.

Jimmy Kennedy

Prompt

Write the story of a disastrous family picnic.

TWISTS

We're home now and all ok. Well, almost all of us are home and most of us are okay. I counted my fingers again. I still had ten of them, for the most part. The little nick out of my index finger made it look concave. I was pretty sure the swelling would go down and I could use it again in the distant future. I would have sat down to reflect on the events of the day, but my backside wasn't quite ready to make contact with any kind of surface. I wondered how hard it would be to sleep standing up. Horses did it so it couldn't be that bad.

This morning was one of the most gorgeous days I'd ever seen. It brought out the poet out in me. The sun, big and orange, was set in a pale blue sky. Shafts of light radiated from the dawn's orb so that it looked like huge astral lollipop with cotton candy hair. What a great day for a family picnic, I couldn't help thinking. I let everyone sleep in a little longer while I finished my coffee. Then I roused my wife and kids and spelled out the day for them. We would drive to Motts Peak and picnic next to the Deerhorn River. We could spend the afternoon hiking and head home around six before the sun dropped behind the mountains. I had already started the smoker so that when we returned it would be to melt in your mouth ribs.

Candace and Charlie loaded their things while Glyn and I took care of the overall needs. We hopped into my shiny new SUV and whistled our fearless dog Barker aboard. That was the last thing that went right. Half way up to Motts Peak a glaring sign notified us that the road was blocked by a slide. Not one to be discouraged by minor inconveniences, I decided to backtrack and take a little known side road, after all that's what four wheel drive vehicles are for. Like I said, the side path was little known … to humans, that is. About a third of the way into my detour we met a family of bears: Mama Bear, Papa Bear and two little hungry Baby Bears all sitting in the middle of the road. They were contentedly eating berries off the vines that spilled onto the narrow path. Making sure that the doors were locked and windows up, I gently tapped my horn at the merry party. They all cast their beady little eyes in our direction for a nanosecond, then returned to their repast. I leaned a little heavier on the horn. Nothing. That was when Barker spotted the feasting bruins and, true to his name, let loose.

I have to hand it to Papa Bear for looking out for his family. He forsook his dinner to investigate the matter as any good patriarch would. He rolled off his haunches and lumbered over to the car. After cocking his head this way and that to take stock of the situation, Papa reared up next to my window. He peered directly at me for a minute or two, then he let out a magnificent roar and started beating my SUV with his paws. In my mind's eye I could see the gashes he was making.

I was just about to back up and leave them in peace when a huge limb fell behind us taking off my bumper. Papa soon was joined by Mama and the kids. Thank God for wives. They know how to state the obvious. Glyn pointed out that now we were trapped in the car with a family of angrybears outside and nowhere to go. It was obvious that the loving bear parents fully intended to overturn us while being cheered on by their brood. Perhaps they wanted to add some meat to go along with the berries. I knew we had to make a run for it.

My next move gave new meaning to the phrase 'off road.' I wrenched the steering wheel hard right and gunned the engine. I think my wife passed out at this point as we careened through the underbrush. More than one innocent forest creature lost its life that day I expect. The kids' terrified cries finally reached my ears and I checked the rear view mirror. Candace was having one of her profuse nosebleeds. It looked like a fountain rigged for a Halloween party. Charlie had covered his eyes and was rocking back and forth. His lips were moving, in prayer, I assume.

.   That was when the brush dwindled and my windshield revealed an open area. I thanked my lucky stars for the clearing until I realized where we were. I was just quick enough with the brakes to keep the entire vehicle from going over the edge. The front wheels hung precariously over the cliff. Below us a very angry Deerhorn River foamed and thundered. At least we had reached our destination, more or less. Glyn woke up from her coma and was just about to get out of the car when I pointed out the inadvisability of that action.

It's funny the things that cross your mind in an emergency. Smoked ribs were sounding pretty good right now, but I pushed them right out of my mind. My family was in need of my direction. By now they were all pretty scared. I pressed a button and the back end of the SUV opened. Like an experienced field commander, I quickly explained the plan. Candace and Charlie would slowly climb over their seats. At the same time Glyn and I would climb over ours towards the rear. Glyn would continue to exit the vehicle while I unstrapped Barker's dog harness. Then the captain and his trusty canine would evacuate the dangling vehicle. Next, we would run like hell away from the cliff.

The best laid plans. Charlie made it over, as did Candace still bleeding profusely. I sent Glyn over her seat to exit the rear with me following close behind. Then I gingerly tried to unharness Barker. His harness was seat belted in and wouldn't budge. His friendly slobbers didn't help matters. I shouted to Glyn and the kids that I couldn't get Barker unstrapped, so I was coming out alone. Their horrified looks scrapped that plan. I remembered my Swiss Army knife. I fished around in my pockets. Of course it wasn't there. In a burst of stupidity I had stuck it in the glove compartment before the trip. Carefully I shifted most of my weight to the back seat while leaning over the front seat to open the glove compartment. Success. I cut Barker loose to the cheers of my adoring family. Man's best friend bolted out the rear so fast that I was flung towards the front seat.

That's when it happened. The car began to teeter-totter, more teetering toward the river than tottering towards the cliff. I said to hell with it, and clutching my knife, jumped out the side door, rolled down the edge ten feet and landed on my backside atop a protruding rock. As I clung to some stubby tree I noticed two things. I had cut a sizeable chunk out of my finger and SUVs don't float, at least not for long. I stared pathetically as it disappeared under the churning water.

Painstakingly I crawled back to the top of the cliff and turned to face my family in triumph. I was alive! We were alive! The mountain hadn't conquered us! The hike home couldn't take too long. This wasn't the Donner Party! They did not share my joy. Four letter words that I had never heard of came rapid fire from Glyn's mouth. Candace was leaning against a tree holding her nose trying to staunch the flow of blood and Charlie was curled up in a fetal position. Barker alone shared my enthusiasm and sprang away among the trees.

Forward into the woods I went with my motley crew straggling

81

behind me, except for Charlie who rolled. Glyn's Tourette's was worse than ever. I was concerned. We trekked as best we could through the thick brush. Before I had a chance to lead them back to civilization we were approached by ten or fifteen natives who had followed our family mutt. Glyn's ode to our family outing ceased abruptly. Candace forgot her nose and Charlie unfurled himself. I have to say it was quite an alarming sight. The natives were friendly at least. We just happened to have strayed into the 'Front and Back to Nature Nudist Colony.' I discovered something: no one should ever become a nudist. It is not a pleasant sight. But fortunately nudity did not prevent them from driving cars. Like I said we're home now except for Barker. He's now a nudist. And by the way, incinerated ribs are not very tasty.

CHAPTER TWENTY-ONE

ROMULUS AT BAY

"I returned, and saw under the sun, that the race is not to the swift, nor the battle to the strong, neither yet bread to the wise, nor yet riches to men of understanding, nor yet favour to men of skill; but time and chance happeneth to them all."

Ecclesiastes 9:11

Prompt

Write a story about this mixed metaphor: 'Revenge is Bliss.'

Whenever we camped I always woke up remembering how much I hated sleeping on the ground. This morning was no different, at least with regard to that. Every part of me ached, including my head. I had to remind myself why I was doing this, and inevitably the answer rushed over me. I'd do anything for my big brother Cadge. "Catch up, catch up. Catch up with your brother, Jimmie" was a phrase I heard Mom say a million times when I was a child. It was no wonder that I thought his name was Cadge. It was the best my two year old enunciation would allow.

I've worshipped Cadge ever since I can remember. We were only a few minutes apart by birth, but that still made me the little brother. My fraternal twin seemed bigger, stronger and smarter. When we were kids I followed him around like a lost sheep. He took it in stride, unless you count the merciless teasing I received at his hands. I didn't mind because it was Cadge doing it. His lopsided smile and gentle cuff on my chin always assured me that it was in fun. I knew that he loved his little brother as much as his little brother loved him. As we grew, the teasing gave way to practical joking. As in everything else, Cadge was a master in this art. First he practiced on me. For a few years I was the habitual target of his tomfoolery, but after that he let me be his partner in crime. More than one hapless classmate or clueless teacher felt the brunt of our combined ingenuity. Yet, no one ever held it against him. He was Cadge.

It is said that time can be a great leveler. In our case, not so much. No matter what strides I made, Cadge was always one up. As teens I was taller; he had more heft. That meant he could beat the crap out of me, or anyone else for that matter. Fortunately, it didn't happen too frequently. In high school he was captain of the football team. I held the same position, only for baseball. Our football team won the state championship every year that he quarterbacked. The baseball team averaged four wins a season my entire career there. I was a lousy pitcher. I excelled in English and the arts; he, in math and computers. The world being what it is, he was the one who garnered all the awards and went on to make millions before he was thirty. I got by well enough on a teacher's salary.

I didn't mind any of that. Cadge wasn't a braggart. He was an 'aw shucks' kind of guy. He deserved the best, and I was always there to

84

support him. But then along came Sherrie Lipton, Mona Lisa as she was known at Ridge High. The competition was on. Each of us tried his best to win her, not without some success. There were sporadic dates with each of us, but they came to nothing. It was inconceivable to me that Sherrie didn't want Cadge. Me, I understood that, but Cadge? Unbelievable. In the end, the three of us graduated and parted, attending three different colleges. But Cadge being Cadge, didn't give up. He eventually won Mona Lisa's heart and hand. Seven years after leaving college they set a date. I would have been broken hearted, except that it was Cadge after all.

Before the engagement, before Cadge left for MIT, and I for Miller College, we made a vow that once we had both graduated from college, we would spend a week together camping every year. It was 'til death us do part, come girlfriends, wives, children, hell or high water. We alternated choosing the places. We've been charged by moose in Maine, almost trampled by bison in Yellowstone and challenged by elk in the Tetons. The Kodiak bears in Alaska we left alone. The sight of the near extinct California condor soaring overhead in the Sonoran Desert is worth almost dying from the heat. The challenges we faced have forged a bond that even Mona Lisa, the miles between us and our divergent careers haven't been able to break.

So when I woke this morning stiff and sore, it was same old same old. Not hearing anything, I assumed Cadge was still asleep. Lying there in the gray dawn, I stretched and automatically reached for my cell, not that there was any reception on Fleabite Mountain. Grope though I did in the pre-dawn light, I couldn't find it. I sat up and looked around. Jesus! Not only was there no phone, there was no backpack either. I tossed aside my blanket. Blanket? Where the hell was my sleeping bag? I jumped to my feet wide awake. It felt like something was crawling over my chest. I gave myself a pat down. No critters, just fringe. Fringe? What the hell was I wearing? Glancing at my attire brought me the revelation that I was wearing buckskins. With great trepidation I looked around for it. Yep. There it was: a coonskin cap lying on the ground. I had turned into Davy Crockett overnight.

I thought by now that the commotion would have wakened Cadge, but he was still out. "Very funny." I thought. He must have drugged me and set me up last night. I was surprised he hadn't gotten up earlier to enjoy the fruit of his labor. I tiptoed over to my sleeping brother in order to shout him awake. Good God. Snuggled under his blanket Cadge was dressed frontier style as well. Now I was scared. I shook him awake with my fringe flapping frantically. He jumped to his feet swearing at me until he took in the same incomprehensible scene: blankets, buckskins, leather pouches, rifles, powder horns. Holy crap! Cadge had picked up the two rifles that lay near our blankets. We were staring blankly at each other when a voice behind us caused us to turn in tandem.

There stood before us a young Native American woman dressed in the fashion of the day. Only her fringe was longer and she had beads on her dress. She might have been very beautiful, but you couldn't tell because deep pock marks disfigured her face. Gift of the white man I though uneasily. We could be in for it.

"Ekoj asi sith." She sounded friendly enough.

Cadge stepped forward while I stood looking like an idiot. Indicating himself by striking his chest, he said, "Cadge."

"This isn't a Tarzan movie, for God's sake." I shouted, but apparently she understood. She mimicked his gesture more gently and said,

"Anorehs."

I joined the Tarzan-style introductions. "James."

She pointed at Cadge and then at me speaking with a very heavy accent, "Ketch. Chemes."

Introductions over, and acknowledging that sign language was the only form of effective communication, we conveyed to her that we were hungry. Smiling she drew a line of freshly caught trout from her pouch. Together we built a fire and cooked the fish. The hard tack that we discovered in our pouches rounded out our morning fare. I shot a 'now what' look at Cadge. He shrugged his shoulders. We needn't have worried. We broke camp and Anorehs beckoned us to follow her. What choice did we have? We had no

86

GPS, not even a compass, so we were helpless. Without technology a local guide was out best bet to get... to get where?

We hiked along a low ridge with a stream to the right. When the sun was straight overhead we stopped for lunch. I can personally vouch that tough, dried, salted unidentified meat is delicious when you are starving. We followed our guide's example and drank from the stream. We filled our canteens such as they were. The stomach of some mammal was my guess. As we proceeded to our destination, wherever that was, Anorehs pointed out birds, insects, animals and plants. She accompanied this with long dissertations on each, none of which we understood. That same clueless feeling I had had when I was on a field trip to a botanical garden at age eight came over me. Our leader was a professor of botany and I thought Latin was his native language. There were plenty of proverbial roses by any other name that all smelled as sweet.

At last we began to descend the ridge. The sun was barely hovering above the mountain horizon. Anorehs stopped. She pointed to a valley below us. Cadge and I stared in wonder. What met our eye was an unbelievable sight. For nestled between two small hills, like a child on its mother's breast was a village of teepees with smoke rising lazily to the darkening sky. It was like something from *The Last of the Mohicans*. Our guide indicated that we needed to make camp for the night. She was right. The sun dropped so quickly behind the ridge we barely had time to make a fire.

As I lay down for the night the gravity of our situation overwhelmed me. Cadge and I had talked off and on during the day. He tried to act all casual and light, but I knew him too well. He was scared. I had never seen my big brother afraid of anything. I think I said my first prayer in twenty years as I dropped into the darkness of slumber.

I woke up the next morning, sore as usual. I was surprised to find the sun high in the sky. I sat up. They were gone. Vanished. Fear gripped my heart. There didn't seem to be any signs of foul play, but she must have kidnapped him. For once in his life being the handsomer, smarter, fitter one served him poorly. I was sick. Abstaining from breakfast, I grabbed my rifle and pouch, saddled the coonskin cap on my head and threaded my way down the ridge to the village.

It took me three hours. I named the path "Lost and Found." It wove sinuously in and out of brush and rocks. By the time I reached the clearing I was bruised by many falls. Any exposed skin was shredded by thorns. I stopped at the edge of the woods and stared at the collection of teepees. They towered over me: neat abodes of tanned hides sewn with animal gut and stretched over wooden frames. How was I supposed to find him among all these? I wasn't equipped to fight a village full of enemies. What did they want with him? A horrible thought came over me. The Anasazi were cannibals. They lived in the Southwest though. I wondered if there had been Native American cannibals in the Appalachians. I crept quietly to the back of the nearest teepee and put my ear to its smooth skin. Apparently some sort of conversation was going on. My heart pounded in my chest. Maybe the fate of my brother was being decided even now.

"…on dung much as it would have been done four hundred years ago before the advent of the European settlers," came a distinctly non-Native American voice.

Stunned I walked around to the flap and opened it. It was filled with a crowd of elementary school students watching an old Native American woman prepare something over a wretched smelling fire.

Being a sharp sort of guy I realized that Cadge had pulled a fast one on me.

***

ONE YEAR LATER

Yosemite National Park

Cadge blinked at the bright sunlight assaulting his eyes. Good God how long had he been asleep? He grabbed his phone. No reception. He looked around. Where the hell was Jimmie?

***

TWISTS

Barbados

I laughed, not without some bitterness, as I remembered last year's trip with Cadge. He had pulled off a pretty solid hoax. I withstood the presumably good natured teasing for a while. Then something snapped inside me. I begin to see my 'big' brother in a different light. All adoration slowly melted as I reflected subjectively on Cadge's behavior throughout his life. He didn't like people, he fed on them. For Cadge everything was about being the center of attention, of getting the glory at the expense of everyone else. His 'aw shucks' humility might inspire others to praise him, but that served his purpose. He ate up the adoration. He would tease cruelly, but all in good fun – for him at least. His retroactive apologies to those he tormented were insincere. A master of manipulation, he would degrade someone so he could raise him up by making him feel included in the fun instead of being the victim. All his nice-guy behavior was as artificial as his contrived smile. If you looked at his eyes you'd see the real motivation behind everything he did. His behavior was guided by an ego that commanded him to control every situation and everyone around him. Cadge was an arrogant, patronizing, self-centered son of a bitch. Four days ago we had set off for Yosemite for our annual camp out.

"Hey handsome." Sherrie handed me a cold beer and sat in the beach chair next to mine. She had reached her conclusions about Cadge about the same time I did.

After closing the teepee flap on dung-lady and her audience, I had strolled around the Muskatawney Native American Reenactment Village pretending to be one of the re-enactors. I figured Cadge had to be somewhere nearby; otherwise, he couldn't fully enjoy his success. I came to the frontier town set at the edge of the village and walked into the saloon. There he was: bathed, clean shaven, sipping beer and waiting for my grand entrance. Sherrie sat next to him. I'll never forget the cool look of superiority that emanated from his face. The taunting that followed was merciless.

"Pretty good, huh? 'Anorehs'... Sherona backwards." He gave his fiance a pinch on the cheek. "Sherrie was a big help. I did a pretty good makeup job on Sherrie Baby. Made a pretty ugly Indian squaw. It was a work of sheer genius. I had a hell of a time getting just the right amount of sedatives into you the first night. It had to be enough so you wouldn't remember the restaging, but not enough to cause you to oversleep, or die," he guffawed. "It all had to look real and like I had nothing to do with it." Cadge roared and leaned back in his chair quaffing his beer..

I joined in with his laughter as I always did, but somehow I didn't feel the way I always had. I sheepishly glanced in Sherrie's direction from time to time during my belittling. Her face had been restored to its usual beauty, but as Cadge ragged on, an expression of disgust replaced her initial smiles. I caught her eye. It was at that moment that our yearlong conspiracy began.

"Thanks, Sherona." I took a draught. "So do you think Cadge has figured it out yet?"

"Oh I imagine so. If not, when he sees his bank account, he'll get it."

"To Cadge." We raised our bottles in an insincere toast, very appropriate to its recipient.

CHAPTER TWENTY-TWO

FOLLOW THE RULES

Prompt

Choose a poem you like. Take the last line and use that line as the first line of your own poem.

(The poem is "The Walrus and the Carpenter," a nonsense poem from *Through the Looking-Glass and What Alice Found There*, by Lewis Carroll. I follow suit with more nonsense.)

91

Follow the Rules

They'd eaten every one,
Although they didn't want to.
But t'was expected of every guest
To dispatch their food quite pronto.

The tribe had certain laws you see,
One of which was this:
Eat what's set before you
Or become a tribal dish.

It wasn't that the natives
Eschewed the guests they'd booked
It's just that they preferred
Their guests be fully cooked.

And so I give you warning
Should you visit Kambi-Kur:
Obey the gastronomic rules
Or end up *soup du jour*.

CHAPTER TWENTY-THREE

THE CRYSTAL INDIAN

"By this, sad Hero, with love unacquainted,
Viewing Leander's face, fell down and fainted."

Christopher Marlowe

Hero and Leander

There was no prompt. The Writer's Group decided to publish a book of ghost stories. I had only been there a couple of months. I dashed this off pretty quickly. It appears in *Tales from the Beyond: An Anthology of the Supernatural*.

ALEXA ANNE KEMPSON

The Kennewiskah

There is a legend about the Kennewiskah Indians – a love story that bears telling. Like so many love stories, it is bittersweet, but the message is well worth repeating: love never dies.

The Kennewiskah people were a small tribe blessed to live in the northern country of Maine where the generosity of nature supplied all that the People could want. There were game and fish aplenty as well as animals to trap for clothing. The Land loved the Kennewiskah People and they loved the Land. There was no want, no disease. There was no war with neighboring tribes, for the Kennewiskah were insignificant and kept to themselves. They had nothing that anyone would want or that the land did not also yield to their neighbors. Yahkmash, the Cold, alone was their enemy, but he was also their friend because he strengthened all who met him in battle each winter and prevailed over him.

They lived in peace along the banks of Lake Manshishkew which in their language means 'the crooked snake.' The lake was shaped like a 'w'. The spit of land, the middle point of the 'w,'" jutted far into the lake, and the Kennewiskah called this northernmost point of the peninsula, Nanwish, 'the Point of Beginning.' The land that fell to its south was where all of the People found their last home. It was their sacred burial ground, Kuhtshwahwish, the Land Beyond. No one spread their tent there, hunted or even trod upon the ground lest they incur the anger of Yahkhitu, the Spirit of the Land Beyond. Only one day a year could this land be traversed and the people set foot on the Point of Beginning. This day was Wewishkah-hen, the Joining Day for maidens and young men. Standing on the holy point of land the Chief would send a flaming arrow through the air to summon his people for this joyous day. Then the Kennewiskah would wend their way through the Sacred Ground to join in the celebration on Nanwish.

Marriages took place only one day a year. All year long young men and

94

maidens who had reached the age of commitment eyed one another and met to talk, well chaperoned by ancient aunts and grandmothers. In preparation for their wedding day the young men and women sought different shores of the lake where they would bathe themselves in the shining clear waters. The purification ritual lasted for seven days. When, at last, the Joining Day arrived a grand parade took place to maidens' tents. Each hopeful groom arrived at his prospective bride's abode with his mother and father. The mother of each young man spoke first with the maiden's mother at the opening. Then she disappeared into her tent to discuss things with her husband. If all was well, the mother reappeared with the dowry which was presented to the mother of the groom. At last all the families met at the bottom of the sacred ground, and they wove their way singing through the burial mounds to the Point of Beginning.

The Eagle Priest conducted the marriage ritual, but the Chief alone could pronounce the final blessing that sealed the marriages. Even the Chief, when he wed, joined the ceremony with all the others until the time of final blessing came. Then he stepped up on the blessing rock and sealed all marriages including his own. Once the blessing was given, the couples returned to their new lodgings and were left alone for seven days. Each day food and gifts from tribe members were brought to them and laid at the doors of their tents.

The greatest and last chief of the Kennewiskah was Hamantush. He took a beautiful maiden, Shamah, as his bride. There was no happier couple than the chief and his princess. For many years their love grew richer and deeper, but they were not blessed with New Life. Year after year they prayed to Mikew, the Spirit of New Life, and to the Great Spirit of All, but no child came. When Shamah approached the age when Nature herself would prevent childbearing she found to her great joy that she was carrying a child. Eagerly the chief and his Princess waited for the spring and the time of New Life.

Hamantush had declared a year of celebration for the coming child. Nature decreed that all her subjects would participate as well. That year the green of the forest was lusher, the autumn more fiery with color, the blue of the lake deeper, the lights of the sky brighter. The wild berries were fat and plentiful beyond telling. To honor the new child, fish threw themselves into the nets of the Kennewiskah. Game strode bravely to meet the arrows of the People. Mahkshaw, the Wolf Spirit, ruled that no predator could enter within the borders of Kennewiskah land. Even Yahkmash, the Cold, dulled his spear to make the winter meek and mild in order to spare Shamah and the baby within her.

Not all of Nature's subjects were pleased to bow to her will. Spring, which the People called Whishaw, was jealous. She had always held the highest place among Nature's subjects. She was the most beautiful and the most anticipated event of all. Now that place of honor fell to Shamah and the time of her birthing. Whishaw rebelled. She plotted with Mikew, the Spirit of New Life, against the mother to be.

Springtime came very late that year. Yahkmash waited and waited. He grew weak and feeble, but the flowers and trees could not bloom without the arrival of Whishaw and Mikew who gave New Life. The month of great flowering arrived, but no blooms adorned the trees or the forest floor or the meadow. Shamah and Hamantush had long anticipated the arrival of their child and could wait no longer. Shamah began the dance of birth without the arrival of Spring and the help of Mikew. She and Hamantush prayed to Mikew to come and assist her, but Whishaw had told her to stay away. Shamah labored and labored, but her child would not come forth to meet Hamantush and the Kennewiskah People. Shamah's strength slipped away from her until she had no more for birthing. She closed her eyes and slept with her child still within her. Yahkhitu came and led her and the child to the Land Beyond.

The Great Spirit was very angry with Wishaw and Mikew. It was too late for Shamah and her child, but the Great Spirit decreed that springtime and new life would never again arrive so late. Birthing and new life would not be delayed in such a malicious way. Whishaw and Mikew hung their heads and obeyed. The Great Spirit ordered the Kahtush lily to come forth, even through the snow, to show the People that springtime would come soon and new life would begin again.

Hamantush was delirious with grief. He trekked to the point of Nanwish to beg for Shamah's return to the land of the living. The women

prepared Shamah's body, but Hamantush would not come. The tribe gathered for their Princess's burial, but their chief refused to attend. They placed Shamah in the Mound of Chieftains. For a week they chanted prayers for her safe passage to the Land Beyond. Hamantush remained at the tip of Nanwish. He bathed himself over and over again in the crystal waters of Lake Manshishkew praying out loud to Yahkhitu to return his bride from the Land Beyond so that they might be joined anew. After many weeks he called the People to him. They were fearful to tread through the sacred burial place since it was not the Joining Day, but they could not refuse the summons of the flaming arrow.

With all the Kennewiskah before him Hamantush spoke.

"My People, I have prayed to Yahkhitu and to the Great Spirit for the return of my beloved Shamah. I know she will come again to me from Beyond and we will begin afresh. Until we embrace there will be no Joinings. Today all the maids and maidens along with the children below the age of hunting will tent themselves upon the sun-setting shores of Lake Manshishkew. The braves above the age of hunting will pitch their abodes upon the sun-rising shores of the Lake. At the bottom of the Sacred Ground the men and women may meet to exchange their game, skins, clothing and wares – such as each camp needs to survive. There must be this separation until Shamah's return. Each day I will purify myself at the Point of Beginning. Shamah will come soon and life will become as always. Marriages will once again sing the song of Beginning and New Life."

But Shamah did not return soon. Day after day, month after month, year after year Hamantush prayed and waited. All day long he bathed himself in the crystal waters in preparation for his bride. As the fishermen paddled by in their canoes they could see only the reflection of the light from the streams of water that poured over the grieving Chief. No one dared to come ashore to console him.

The children grew and there were no more to replace them. The young maidens grew older and passed the age of bearing. Though the Land yielded to them food and the People lived in peace, their numbers lessened each year. The grieving Hamantush took no notice. All day and all night he poured the shining waters upon himself. Long after the last of the

97

Kennewiskah had died and lay in Kuhtshwahwish, their last chief continued his lustrations, his body shining like the crystal waters of Lake Manshishkew.

Centuries passed. The point of Nanwish and the entire peninsula where the Kennewiskah people slept forever came to be known as Indian Point to the white settlers who had invaded the land. Many who paddled the waters of the Lake have seen the shape of a human bathed in crystal light of reflected waters. Day or night the translucent figure can be seen glistening eerily against the deep green of the forest. The legend of the Crystal Indian was passed down generation to generation in order to warn people from this sacred land. Those who attempted to traverse the peninsula disappeared and never returned. The same misfortune befell anyone who tried to beach their craft on Indian Point. The bones of old boats can be seen upon its shores, and it is assumed that the bones of those who brought them there lay, invisible, among their wreckage. From time to time many who live near Indian Point observe a tremendous light fill the sky. This, they say, is the wrath of Hamantush visited upon anyone who profanes Kuhtshwahwish and Nanwish.

***

The Hermit of Indian Point

It may have been desire to escape civilization that propelled the old man into the wilderness. No one ever knew for sure. Hugh had worked decades in Boston in his family's fishing enterprise. So committed was he to Mann Fisheries that he never wed and had no children. One day for no reason apparent to those knew him, he turned his back on his business, family, friends and his prosperity. With only the clothes on his back and a walking staff in hand he headed north. It is said that he walked northward forty days and nights until his path was blocked by a beautiful shining body of water. He had reached Lake Manshishkew. When he arrived at the northernmost point of a spit of land that jutted into the Lake and could go no farther, he stopped, lay down and slept. There Hugh raised a small cabin and lived alone.

The town folk in the village of Kennewiskah heard that a stranger had invaded Indian Point, but no one had witnessed the event. For years everyone assumed he was but another casualty of the Crystal Indian. Then one day a tall scraggly-bearded figure strode into the small town to purchase some amenities of civilization. With barely a word to anyone, he left and disappeared into the woods of the forbidden peninsula. He repeated this procedure every few years. He was known to Kennewiskans as the Hermit of Indian Point.

***

Déjà vu

The fierce rain had ceased and the clouds had begun to disperse. Remnants scuttled along the dark sky to reveal the full orb of a blood-red moon. It looked angrily down on the earth like the Cyclops' eye pierced by Odysseus' spear. Samantha pulled her jacket tighter around her, but to no avail. The wind easily tore through it and cut to her bones. Her eyes were burning and her cheeks chafed red. It was, after all, late October in northern Maine, and bitter winds always arrived early to announce winter's impending brutality.

She trekked onward through alternating patches of amber light and pitch darkness, both of them dictated by the dance between the clouds and the moon high above her. The unreliability of steady light and the frigid winds impeded her progress to the hermitage on Indian Point. Only thoughts of being back home wrapped in a thick wool blanket in front of a warm fire and gulping a mug of steaming cider kept her going.

Why Samantha had felt it necessary to go out this night was a puzzle. There was no substantive reason whatsoever. After she had prepared and eaten late dinner, she sat stroking Mikew who was curled contentedly on her lap. It had been their nightly ritual since she could remember. Gray haired Samantha cooed at her snow white cat, and the ball of cotton fluff purred back. Samantha was deeply engaged in this dialogue when it happened: an irresistible urge to go check on the Hermit.

All her life the elderly woman had heard about the mysterious Hermit. She had never actually seen him and often wondered if the stories the

99

villagers told were true. They had ranged from his being a former businessman gone insane to his being an escaped convict. Many whispered he had had five or six wives whom he had killed and buried on Indian Point. She shuddered at the thought of the latter; nevertheless, she forced herself into her jacket and headed for whatever fate was to meet her at Indian Point.

Normally the walk would have been an easy one even at night. But tonight was different. It was as if all of nature had mustered forces to work against her. This only impelled her to press on with all her strength. The sooner she got there, the sooner she could return home. She leaned in against the gale and picked up her pace. The wind grew icier with every step. She couldn't feel her face at all. At the top of the hill she took the full brunt of nature's fury. Saplings driven mad, either by the moon or the winds, whipped around her in a frenzy. Their vicious fingers reached out and scratched her right cheek. Samantha uttered a cry and tucked her head down to deflect any further attack. She began to wonder if all the stories of the forbidden burial ground were true. She continued treading carefully down the steep grade keeping her eyes fixed on the rocky path.

Halfway down the hill a bloodcurdling scream penetrated the night. It froze Samantha more surely than any wind could have done. A hungry owl swooped down in front of her to snatch its hapless prey. A bad omen. Looking up she could now see the top of a ramshackle cabin at the foot of the hill. Despite the shack being half hidden in a copse of Balsam firs, a warm yellow glow escaped from the small mullioned windows. It lifted her spirits and at the same time caused her consternation. What nonsense to have come. All must be well with the old recluse. She turned to go back to her cottage, but she could not. Terror flooded her being. It was as if unseen hands held her in a vice. The wind propelled her down the hill. She pitched forward into the night.

Closer and closer she drew to the cabin. A strange feeling began to overtake her fear. She ought to be afraid, terrified, but she was not anymore. Anger? It would have been logical to be angry. Likely as not, she was on a fool's errand. She was bound to be greeted by an old, malodorous misanthrope who would send her home without offering her the warmth of a fire and a cup of hot coffee. Curiosity? No, oddly enough she knew if she searched deep inside herself she would find the answer. Could it be that the Hermit was dead and she was headed there to bring this news to the people of Kennewiskah so that he might be properly buried? Yet she knew he was not dead, but waiting, waiting for her. Again fear rose within her. She pushed it aside as the unseen hands continued to guide her forward. She shivered. Now she was cold through and through. Familiarity? That was it! She had an odd feeling of having done this all before.

Samantha reached the yard. The cabin lay directly before her with the first rays of dawn glancing off the thick window panes. The glare was slightly blinding so she shaded her eyes as her foot touched the bottom step. When she reached the top the door opened, unbidden. How strange! With all the noise from the wind there was no way the Hermit could have heard her approach. A blinding light filled the doorway. At last Samantha Cooper had arrived.

***

The Beginning of the End

The Hermit had spent a restless night and risen early in the morning. His bones ached a little from all the rain, but it was over now. Last night had been wretched indeed! A storm to rival anything he had seen in his eighty plus years. He glanced at the paucity of wood next to the fireplace and decided to fetch a load from the woodpile as soon as dawn broke. It would need some time to dry out if he were to have a decent fire today. He contemplated the waters of the Lake that, even by the dwindling moonlight, shone like glass. He finished the breakfast things and dried the last plate. It was still dark, but by instinct he knew the first ray of light was about to show itself. Wiping his knobby fingers on the cloth that hung next to the sink, the Hermit flung on an old sweater and headed for the door. He whistled to Eagle who rose stiffly from his bed and followed his master in order to assist him in whatever duties were planned for the day.

He flung the door open. It was the last thing Hugh Mann ever did.

101

***

The End of the Beginning

"I can't make anything out of it." The freshman deputy stood on the cabin porch looking down on a bizarre scene.

The two bodies that reposed there were as different as could be. Samantha Cooper looked as though she'd seen a ghost. Her face was frozen in utter surprise. She lay stiff as a board, arms by her side, face up on the Hermit's porch. Her eyes were wide open and fixed as if on some distant object that defied recognition. At her head sat a fat white cat nonchalantly licking its paws and twitching its tail as though guarding a dead mistress were par for the course. In front of the frozen spinster, right on the door's threshold, the old Hermit was arranged in a heap – like someone had let the air out of him and he just deflated. A grey wolf-dog sat board-straight next to the puddle that was his master. He panted with expectation for the next command. His master's face, unlike the woman's, was as serene as one of the corpses in Ebenezer Jenkin's Funeral Home. Eb knew how to make his 'folk' look like they were very happy to be dead and in their coffins. They looked so fully absorbed with being dead you almost wanted to hang a 'Do Not Disturb' sign on them. Burying them seemed an intrusion.

"It's finally happened." Old Sheriff Hawke smiled at the youngster. "It's the Crystal Indian. Looks like he finally found his bride."

ABOUT THE AUTHOR

Alexa Anne Kempson is the author of the Manawassa Series of mysteries. She resides in De Funiak Springs, Florida. Raised in nearby Pensacola, she returned to Northwest Florida after a 40 year absence. She lives in an historic house, "The Pansy Cottage," on the perfectly circular Lake Defuniak. She is a magna cum laude graduate of Duke University with graduate work at Duke and at the University of Iowa in the area of Old and New Testaments and Intertestamental Studies. She has five grown children and five grandchildren.

Made in the USA
Charleston, SC
30 March 2015